CW00924288

The Dartford Destroyer

The Life and Career of Dave Charnley
British, Empire and European Champion

Jim Kirkwood

Foreword by Norman Giller

Dalcumly Press

First published in the UK in 2011

Dalcumly Press
10 Forest Grove
Kilmarnock, Ayshire KA3 1UP

ISBN 978-0-9569253-0-5

Papers used in this book are natural, renewable and recyclable products sourced from well-managed forests and certified in acordance with the rules of the Forest Stewardship Council.

Typeset in Adobe Garamond, designed and produced by Gilmour Print, www.gilmourprint.co.uk

This book is dedicated to the late William and Nellie Charnley, father and mother to William, Dave, Joe and Isabella. They made the move from Craigneuk to Dartford in 1935 hoping that their family would prosper. They didn't live to appreciate fully the fruits of that momentous decision, but their offspring have carved out successful lives for themselves in their own particular way.

Contents

Foreward

Dave Charnley is long overdue this revealing tribute book by boxing aficionado Jim Kirkwood. Anybody of a certain age will confirm that Dave was one of the greatest British fighters never to win a world championship, and he deserves acclaim and appreciation as he approaches his mid-seventies.

This was certainly the view of my best friend, the late Terry Lawless, who knew a thing or three about what goes into the making of a champion. We once drew up a list of the ten finest British boxers not to win a world title.

On the list: Nel Tarleton, Harry Corbett, Jack Hood, Tommy Farr, Jock McAvoy, Ernie Roderick, Peter Keenan, Henry Cooper, Brian Curvis, and top of the tree, Dave Charnley.

I was a young reporter on the trade newspaper Boxing News when Dave, 'The Dartford Destroyer', was at his peak, and I was ringside when he was the victim of a miscarriage of justice in his second world title fight against Joe 'Old Bones' Brown. To this day I will never know how Tommy Little failed to hold up the Kent man's hand at the end of a pulsating fight. The vast Earls Court crowd agreed with my assessment, and the booing, jeering and near riots went on for more than half an hour. There is a graphic reconstruction of the momentous fight on the following pages.

This was British fair play gone mad. In any other country in the world the points decision would have gone to the hometown boy, who fought his heart out and more than matched the adroit, flashy Brown for skill and effort.

Dave gave the performance of his life that night, and could not hide his disappointment in defeat. But, as always, he was dignified and did not get involved in mud slinging.

Jim Kirkwood expertly paints a portrait of Dave in this book that captures his dedication, discipline and his will to win. If he had been fighting in these days of silly money, he would have earned millions with his fists.

I have rarely seen a more compact fighter than Charnley. There were no chinks in his defence, and he fired combination punches with blinding speed, and when he planted his feet was as heavy a puncher as any lightweight produced on these shores. His thumping right southpaw lead was his foundation punch, and he would follow up with buzzsaw punches that had his opponents nonplussed. He could take the lead, but was happiest and at his most dangerous when counter punching.

There was a tendency for him to be cautious in the opening rounds, pacing himself and *casing* his opponent like a deadly assassin waiting for the right moment to take out his target. He was a connoisseur of controlled violence and had a poker face that rarely showed what he was thinking in the ring.

As a boxing PR who worked with Muhammad Ali and most of the top British fighters of the 1970s/early 1980s, I felt Dave was not given the projection he warranted outside the small world of Dartford. He was a local hero, but should have been a national treasure.

His pugnacious manager Arthur Boggis always came across to me as a suspicious man, almost jealously determined to keep Dave away from the media spotlight rather than giving him the publicity build-up his talent merited.

Anybody reading this well-researched and informative biography will wonder what Dave could have achieved had he shifted his headquarters to London and courted the press. It worked for Jim Watt a couple of decades later when he came under the Terry Lawless wing and almost overnight became a world champion rather than Jim Who?

Charnley against Ken Buchanan or Jim Watt would have been a fight worth walking a million miles to see.

And, as you are about to read, all three leading lights were proud Scots, even though Dave was born in Kent.

Thanks for the memories, Dave, and I hope Jim Kirkwood's conscientiously compiled biography brings your exploits to the attention of a new generation. For us old gits, you were pretty special, and you were always an admirable advertisement for the better face of boxing.

Seconds out . . . here comes an excellent read about an exceptional fighter. Enjoy!

***Norman Giller** is a sports historian whose 89th book will be the complete record of the life and times of Henry Cooper, the boxer and the man.*

Acknowledgements

First and foremost it has to be appreciated that this book would have been very difficult to write without the co-operation of the Charnley family. Modest to the end Dave had to be press-ganged into giving the go-ahead but once committed he provided valuable assistance. Brothers Joe, and William, gave willingly of their time as did sister Isabella, Dave's wife Maureen and daughters Lisa and Joanna.

The journey started in Motherwell where school friend, Billy Reid, gathered the Craigneuk contingent for an interview session in his home. Mrs Reid supplied the tea and cakes for cousins Jim and John King, Henry Ralston and Annie Peat. Friends Alex Whyte and Allan Haddow were also fed and watered.

Within days of committing myself to the project I received immediate help and guidance from authors Bob Mee and Bob Lonkhurst making me feel not quite so lonely. Ex-train driver, Arthur Ellison from Liverpool, took the time to send me his meticulously maintained Dave Charnley scrapbooks to which I often referred.

Grateful thanks go to former freelance photographer, Derek Rowe. Derek was at ringside for all the big fights in London during the period of Dave's career because, allegedly, he was the only photographer possessing an evening suit, a requirement in those days! Derek has given me kind permission to use several photos for the book, including the one on the dust wrapper. It's amazing what computers can do. Derek's photo of Dave, which was taken on black and white film, has been professionally *coloured* by Robert Brown who owns Unforgettable in Irvine. I'm sure you'll agree he's a wizard with his electronic paintbrush! Equally important was the practical assistance Derek gave me concerning some of the characters and locations back in the day. He was always available to assist and is one of life's true gentlemen.

Former sparring partners Bob Paget, Terry Rees and Larry O'Connell described how it felt to be hit by Dave and were able to provide an interesting insight into the London boxing scene. Another ex-fighter, Derry Treanor, knew Dave well and both shared the same manager, Arthur Boggis. Derry was able to provide a different perspective on the character of Boggis. The only opponent I traced was, Sammy McCarthy, who described in graphic detail the after-effects of a Charnley rib-bender. Modern day *cut-man*, Benny King also helped with an insight into the skills of Joe Brown through days of sparring with the great man.

Chas Taylor, a member of the London Ex-Boxers Association, kindly gave up his time and invited Dave and I to his house where we enjoyed looking at several important items relating to Dave's career. Chas also went out of his way to assist me with contact details and anecdotal information from this era.

Can any boxing book be written without some input from Harold Alderman MBE? Harold put himself out regularly to assist, and I am very grateful.

Of course, the bulk of my research was carried out using

articles from the national newspapers including the Daily Mail, Daily Telegraph, Daily Express, Evening News and the Daily Mirror. I am grateful to the leading boxing journalists of the time who wrote in the national press. Foremost amongst these were Harry Carpenter, Reg Gutteridge, Peter Wilson, Donald Saunders, Desmond Hackett, Sydney Hulls, Peter Butler and others too numerous to mention. But I found the reports of Donald Saunders to be written in a style which suited my purpose best and I drew on his work more regularly. Having said all that, the good old Boxing News was indispensable. It really is the *Hansard* equivalent for British boxing. I would certainly have struggled but for their coverage during the years of Dave's career. In the same vein, the modern day website, www.boxrec.com, provided me with detailed information on the records of most of Dave's opponents.

Dave was such a hero in Dartford that it is no surprise that two Dartford men, Richard Drew and Tom Brown, have provided so much help with local knowledge and a sense of just how much his success meant to the town.

Maureen Cottle, wife of Dave's late friend, George, willingly gave up her time to provide much background information on Dave's life, particularly after he retired from boxing, as did business associate, Alan Parnell. Bernard Hart, former proprietor of Lonsdale Sports, also chipped in with background details from that period.

I would have loved it if Jack Solomons, Arthur Boggis, and especially Ray Bartlett, had still been with us –what stories they could have given me.

Finally, I have pleasure in publicly thanking Norman Giller

for his foreward. I asked Norman if he could do it, and less than 24 hours later, while suffering from a stomach upset, around 750 words of sheer class had arrived on my computer. It put the efforts of your poor novice author to shame.

Finally, and most importantly, can I record my sincere thanks to my wife, Edna, and nephew, Gavin, for their patience in pouring over my work to ensure that there were as few grammatical errors as possible.

Jim Kirkwood
Kilmarnock, 2011

Introduction

The career defining fight for Dave Charnley was in April 1961 when he fought Joe Brown at Earls Court, London for the world lightweight title. Having lost his first attempt to the same man two years previously in Texas, this was the opportunity to stamp his name for ever in the history of professional boxing. This fight took place long before the advent of live coverage of sporting events, but was shown on the BBC the following evening.

18,000 fans from all over Britain made their way to the London venue including approximately 3,000 alone from Dave's hometown of Dartford. Car ownership was still not common so public transport was the order of the day. The vicinity of the arena therefore teemed with people on foot, milling around excitedly discussing how the fight would go. Once inside, the first surprise for the modern day sports fan would be an awareness of just how smokey the atmosphere was in those far off days before the No Smoking ban appeared.

The vast majority of those in attendance had never seen Joe Brown fighting. All they could base any judgements they had on his abilities was from newspaper or magazine reports plus comments from those who had actually seen him in action. However, all these people had seen the Dartford Destroyer in action before, and for them, that was enough! He was a *come forward*, hard punching threshing machine who tended to scythe down opponents with regularity. He was not just the champion of Britain, Europe and the Empire but had outboxed and outfought the best that America had to offer, with only a few exceptions. Foremost amongst this number was Carlos Ortiz, but to the loyal Charnley fan club excuses for that setback came readily to mind. After all had not Dave fought the Puerto Rican with pain killing injections in both hands?

When the fanfares sounded and the searchlights found the boxers as they made their way to the ringside, the entire crowd rose to their feet as one. The eager anticipation of the crowning of Britain's new world champion, may at this point have begun to diminish for some, as they began to realise the enormity of the task Dave faced. When the announcer began his ritual, the tall coloured American moved about restlessly as the local lad sat impassively on his corner stool, still in his dressing gown given to him by the famous entertainer, Billy Cotton.

One hour later, following a points defeat, Dave looked out of the ring, not at smiling faces and hand clapping from fans who thought he had made a courageous attempt to win the title, but at a virtual riot. Stewards and police were rushing onto the ring apron to protect referee, Tommy Little, the sole arbiter for the fight, who had scored against Dave. The Fulham newsagent had brought the house down with his decision. Programmes, cigarette lighters and coins rained into the ring as scuffles broke out with more sensible fans restraining their friends from rushing towards the ring. The booing and jeering seemed to cause a vibration right through the arena and all Dave could do was hang his head. His eyes filled with tears when he realised that the constant, daily, training regime he had committed himself to for over ten years, and all the hand and eye injuries he had borne, to get to this pinnacle, had all been in vain. He would much preferred to have been knocked out cleanly or hammered from pillar to post in such a way that was so conclusive that a defeat would have been the inevitable outcome. But believing he had won, an albeit close decision, and to have his hopes ripped out from under his feet was too much to bear.

Many respected boxing people claim that Dave Charnley was the best British boxer NEVER to have won a world title, and this epithet is simultaneously huge praise, and a huge disappointment. Most of us lead fairly anonymous lives and we have our own private successes and failures, but we don't usually experience the massive frustrations that come with *almost* reaching the very top.

Many of the boxing trophies he won are still with him but until this book started its journey from research to conclusion, they remained in a bin liner bag placed in his loft. His devoted wife, Maureen, had often gently suggested that he should have them out on display so that visitors could see how successful he had been, but Dave thought this would have seemed boastful. If he had beaten Brown that night he would have had no material items to remember it by anyway, because championship belts were not presented for world title fights in those days.

In 2009, trade paper the Boxing News, brought out a magazine to celebrate its centenary. They called the period from 1940 to 1969 the Golden Era for boxing. They carefully selected Britain's five best boxers during this time. They considered the best to have been Randolph Turpin who won the world middleweight title from possibly the greatest boxer of all time, Sugar Ray Robinson. Second was Welshman, Howard Winstone who had held a version of the world featherweight crown. Third was Freddie Mills the former world light heavyweight champ and fifth was Scotsman Jackie Paterson who held the world flyweight crown from 1943 to 1948. Dave was placed fourth in this list, and you will immediately notice that he is the only one of this elite group who did not win a world title.

Turpin, Winstone, Mills and Paterson were not this country's only world champions of course because Rinty Monaghan, Johnny Caldwell, Terry Allen, Terry Downes and Walter McGowan could have been added. Others, who like Dave, just fell short, might also have been included. Therefore this acknowledgement from the Boxing News was praise indeed and emphasized just how high a regard the boxing public had for the Dartford born fighter.

So many knowledgeable boxing people have came out and stated that Dave was the best boxer since the Second World War NOT to have won a world title that this label seems to have become an established term whenever the name, Dave Charnley, is mentioned. Highly respected London trainer Terry Lawless, who took Frank Bruno, Jim Watt, Charlie Magri and Maurice Hope to world titles used this term in a 1980 interview with the Sunday People and it seems to have stuck. Mickey Duff who has been involved in almost every role in boxing from fighter to promoter has often said the same thing. These were nice compliments and have high value but are they really much consolation when you are a born winner?

Dave comes from good West of Scotland working class stock, and as a boxer clearly showed some of the personality traits which epitomised people from that part of the world. He was extremely hard working, training almost every day during his ten year professional career. He was determined to win no matter who he fought, but also very modest with regard to the successes he had. He shied away from the publicity which followed him and became easily embarrassed by it all.

Today Dave lives quietly with his wife Maureen in the quiet Kent countryside. None of his neighbours, nor anyone else in the town he has lived in for almost ten years have any idea who he is. We can be sure that this is the way he likes it. If you were invited into his home you would see nothing of the illustrious sporting career to remind you that every national newspaper in the country once covered in huge detail the build ups, the fights, and the aftermaths, and his thousands of fans up and down the country read every word.

This story will take you through the Charnley family history and how they came to be based in Dartford. It will describe Dave's successful amateur career which laid the foundations for what was to come. His professional fights from when he started, until he retired, still as undefeated British lightweight champion, will be described in detail. We will end the journey by looking at his life after boxing and how he now enjoys the quiet life, surrounded by family and friends.

CHAPTER 1

From Craigneuk to Dartford

When Sam Charnley transferred from York City to Dartford Football Club, in the Southern League, he would have had no idea that as a result of this move his nephew would go on to be known throughout the length and breadth of the country as the 'Dartford Destroyer'.

By the time David Fraser Charnley came into this world on 10 October 1935, Sam had organised houses and jobs in Dartford for his own parents, his sister Annie and her husband Jimmy Shaw, his brother Joe and his wife and Dave's parents William and Nellie. The men got employment with London Papermills courtesy of officials at Dartford FC while Sam continued to ply his own trade as centre-half for the club. Sam had played the game at the highest level appearing in the first team on 55 occasions for Wolverhampton Wanderers.

William and Nellie like the rest of their families came from the village of Craigneuk near Motherwell, and were proud Scots. Williams' mother Annie originated from Derbyshire, but the Charnley heritage is not so clear. The Fraser side of the family though were firmly rooted in Craigneuk. Nellie's father, David, was very well known locally due to his work as a *rag and bone* man. He could be seen touring the area daily with his horse and cart picking up items which he could later sell at a profit. Mother Isabella, or Bella as she was known, was a member of the large Ralston family and was at one time the Worthy Mistress of the local womens section of the Orange Order. In later years when Dave's fights were being transmitted live on the radio, grandfather David would walk round and round the village while Bella sat listening intently as the contests progressed. When he saw his wife standing outside he would realise the fight was over and more often than not he would know the result due to the smile on her face but his only response was to ask if Dave had been hurt in any way.

When William and Nellie married in 1932 the principal employment for men in the area was in the local steel works, and William worked in a firm called Clyde Alloys. Like his brother Sam, he was also a reasonable footballer and played at that time for Wishaw Juniors. Their first son, William, came along in 1933, and before the arrival of Dave, Uncle Sam had managed to find the family a house at 86 The Brent, Dartford. In those far off days before the prevalence of cars, motorways and efficient methods of communication, we can only imagine the concerns of the young couple. As migrating Scots however, they were not alone. Thousands had passed this road before them arriving mostly in places like Corby which subsequently became known as 'Little Scotland'. Dartford and the surrounding area also saw the arrival of other Scots so they might not have felt as isolated as we might have expected.

However the Charnley household, like thousands of others could not have foreseen the nightmare looming just around the corner. In September 1939 Britain declared war on Germany, and almost immediately dad William was conscripted into the army, where he was to remain for the entire duration of the war.

1940 started well for the family, when in January a third son, Joe, was born, but this joy was not to last. Dartford being situated close to important sea ports and heavy engineering works was a prime target for German bombing raids. The first disaster arrived when a German bomb led to the untimely death of Dave's paternal grandfather, William. This was soon followed by the destruction of the family home during another Luftwaffe bombing raid. Nellie and her three sons were suddenly homeless, and while there can be little doubt that the extended family would have gladly took the family in, Nellie made probably the safest decision, and took her flock back up to Craigneuk.

They were welcomed with open arms and initially resided downstairs from grandparents David and Bella, with Nellie's uncle and his wife, Henry and Sarah Ralston. A short time later they got their own accommodation in a flat owned by a local businessman called Mc Ivor in Meadowhead Road. Older brother William and Dave were soon enrolled in the local Craigneuk Public School, and this was to be their life for the next five years. This was a fairly routine period for the evacuated Charnley family and they were recognised as just another local family with any trace of English accents from William and Dave being quickly lost. In 1943 Nellie and William must have been pleased when a daughter arrived in April. She was christened Isabella after her grandmother Fraser.

When the war was coming to a close in 1945, Nellie and William made the critical decision to stick with their original plan for the future, and the family moved back down to Dartford where they were accommodated with grandmother,

Annie at 32 East Hill. Dave attended Dartford East County Secondary school and with his Scottish background soon earned himself the nickname 'Jock'. This fact was to lead to his first boxing defeat! A teacher came across a fight in the school playground between Dave and another lad, so in good 1940's style the teacher brought them into the gym, gave them boxing gloves, and instructed them to sort out their differences properly. The fight was stopped when Dave was receiving a pummelling.

This was not the only trouble Dave got into in those days. Both Dave and his pal Malcolm Dolden found themselves banned from a swimming pontoon in Dartford when they turned up wearing a pair of schoolgirl's knickers which they had stolen off a close line, belonging to Malcolm's sisters, Daphne and Gillian!

Now firmly settled in school, it became clear that Dave's future success would more likely stem from the sporting arena than from the classroom. He was a keen sportsman and performed well in football and cricket, representing the school at both. But it is in another sport that Dave became much better known. Close to grandmother Annie's house was a scout hut situated in Little Queen Street, which for part of the time was used by the Dartford and District Amateur Boxing Club. One day, Dave, along with older brother William, were walking past the hut when they could hear the sort of noises you would expect from a boxing club. Both youngsters, being curious, peered into the hall through a crack in one of the wooden walls. Dave saw a classmate whom he knew was the Kent schoolboy champion. He told William that he could beat the lad easily. Just at that an old gentleman from the club, Bob Lloyd, caught them and asked them if they wanted to come in.

Once inside Mr Lloyd instructed both boys to try to skip like the others, and then told them to practice *fighting* in front of the large mirrors. After a while William and Dave were asked if they wanted to go into the makeshift ring to spar with one of the boxers. William quickly answered in the negative but Dave was a bit more confident and accepted the offer. He was put in with his classmate and was quickly hammering him around the ring. Mr Lloyd, beginning to show more interest, selected another young boxer who received similar treatment. Eventually, a 17 year old, Henry Carey, six years Dave's senior, took up the sparring session and only then was the youngster's progress halted. Afterwards William overheard Carey telling Mr Lloyd that it had taken all his experience to control Dave. The 11 year old had caught the boxing bug and became a regular at the club.

The scout hut, when being used as a boxing gym, had all the necessary equipment, with medicine balls, boxing gloves, mirrors, punchbags and of course the ring which consisted of lengths of rope held together by corner posts fixed into the floor. At the end of each nights work this all had to be put away ready for use by the scouts the following night. In those far off days it might be considered surprising that Bob Lloyd, his assistant Frank Sharpe and matchmaker Buddy Pett, also provided boxing facilities for troubled youngsters from a nearby Borstal institution. These men obviously decided that they had a responsibility to help youngsters achieve a level of fitness and discipline which was missing at that stage in their lives. Young

Dave was too young to fully appreciate the benefits which could arise from such an initiative, and admits he did not like the experience of mixing with these lads.

Soon after joining, Dave's first fight was arranged and William mentioned this to their father. Like most dads, he was a bit concerned that his boy was going to get hurt so he popped round to the scout hut to speak to Bob Lloyd. At this extremely early stage in Dave's boxing career, the elderly boxing instructor had some prophetic words for Mr Charnley when he said that 'I think we have a potential world champion here!'.

Dave's fledgling boxing career almost ground to a halt some months later. On returning from a fight at Godalming one night, a bus the boxing club had hired, broke down just outside Dartford and Dave was left to walk a couple of miles to his home. His mother, Nellie, was not pleased and banned him from the club. After a few weeks absence Mr Lloyd sent his son round to the Charnley family home in an effort to persuade Mrs Charnley to let her son continue fighting. She was having none of it and told young Lloyd that she didn't want her son's face bashed up. Lloyd junior asked Nellie if she could see any marks on his face, to which she replied that she couldn't. He then said that he had taken part in 50 fights, and having given some thought to this, she rather reluctantly gave her permission for Dave to return to the club. It later transpired that young Lloyd had never had a fight in his life!

At a boxing show held within J and E Halls factory in 1948, the best fight of the night was a Class A junior contest between two 13 year olds, Dave Charnley from the local Dartford club and H Cornish of Swanley. Charnley attacked from start to finish and won the fight. Both lads received a standing ovation from the fans. The following year, this time at the Drill Hall in Bexleyheath, young Dave stopped 15 year old J Linton from Medway winning in the 2nd round. Both of these early contests demonstrated that even at this stage Charnley was an exciting, attacking fighter.

During the 1948-49 boxing season, Dave, weighing between 5st 8lb and 6st 1lb, won firstly the Gravesend and Northfleet Schools Amateur Boxing Association sectional championships before losing in the final of the Kent Schools competition. As was the custom in those days Dartford East County school awarded Dave the *school colours* for representing them with distinction.

The following season, now a weight higher at 7st 2lb, Dave went one better. After winning the Gravesend and Northfleet qualifying round, he won the Kent Schoolboys title and again received his *colours* from the school. After winning this championship Dave fought the South East London champion, Ken Margerium of Downham at Oakwood Pavilion in Crayford. Local newspapers reported that on beating Margerium, Charnley had won 29th successive contests.

Dave was now 15 years old and his schooling had came to an end. Soon afterwards he was apprenticed as a boilermaker with Vickers – Armstrong Engineering works in nearby Crayford and his boxing career continued without interruption.

However, a life changing tragedy was on the horizon. Mother Nellie became ill and quickly succumbed to a brain tumour. As could be imagined the whole family was devastated. The sorrow that this brought has never left Dave and even today, sixty years later, he chokes with emotion when talking about it. Nellie was an extremely strong character and was clearly the cement which bound the family together. Dad William, while holding down a full-time job, now at J and E Halls factory, had the prospect of looking after sons William, Dave, Joe and daughter Isabella on his own. William and Dave were now in work, but Joe, aged 10 years and sister Isabella aged 7 were school children. Once again relatives waded in to help out and the family struggled on. Perhaps Dave's future dedication to training and his will to win was his way of dealing with the sadness?

Young Charnley then embarked on the qualifying process for the Amateur Boxing Association Youth Championships of Great Britain. On the 6 January 1951 he won the Kent junior title at 8st 7lb and three weeks later annexed the Southern Counties championship at Hove in Sussex. In the quarter finals held at Reading, Dave stopped Home Counties champion G Moy of Hitchin Youth Club in the 3rd round. At the finals held in the Royal Albert Hall on the 2nd of March Dave finished as runner up when he was outpointed by R D Skinner of the Caius club in London.

But like Dave's previous efforts to win the Kent schoolboys title, his second attempt at the British championships was to prove successful. His challenge started at Maidstone on the 15 December 1951 when he won the Kent 9st title. On 12 January, once again at Hove, he won the Southern Counties section, going on to beat the Home Counties representative a month later. At the Royal Albert Hall in the afternoon Dave beat M D de Courey Whewell of the Bold Boxing Academy who was representing the Northern Counties. Whewell had won his three previous contests by first round knockouts and both boxers started cautiously. By the 3rd round Charnley's body shots had taken their toll and were to win him the fight. That same evening Dave fought L Wilson of Camberwell who had won his semi-final via a first round knockout. Wilson stormed out at the first bell and tried to end the contest quickly. However as the fight wore on Charnley got on top and won a narrow decision. Also that day the Dartford club's Maurice Longhurst lost in his semi-final.

For some unknown reason the Dartford club was winding down at this time, but a man who was to have a significant influence on Dave's boxing career came on the scene. Ray Bartlett had noticed the young Charnley boxing on a J and E Halls show and had not forgotten how impressed he had been. When he learned about the impending demise of the local club, he approached Dave and suggested that if he wanted to continue his improvement he would have to travel to London. Ray was the matchmaker for the famous Fitzroy Lodge club whose premises were situated under the railway arches in Lambeth. During discussions with Ray, Dave made it clear that he would not consider changing from his natural southpaw stance. In those days many boxing pundits considered that those intent on fighting with their right foot and right hand forward should be shot at birth. What is surprising is that the shy, slightly introverted Charnley should be so assertive on this issue.

Dave got his way however, and the move to the Fitzroy went through without a hitch.

Dave always liked Ray, who would be with him throughout his entire boxing career. Bartlett was a newspaper vendor who had a pitch near St Pauls Cathedral in Central London. According to those who knew him, he was a shabbily dressed character, and this provoked the well known journalist Reg Gutteridge to publicly announce rather unkindly during a dinner that he had spotted a new phenomenon – Ray Bartlett had changed his shirt! What was abundantly clear however was that Ray was not shabby in the memory department. In those pre-computer and internet days, he had a detailed knowledge of boxers across the globe which was second to none. Freelance photographer Derek Rowe remembers being asked regularly by Ray to record details of fights and fighters at shows he was unable to attend. The value of this kind of knowledge in terms of matchmaking and identifying sparring partners cannot be overstated. In future years there would be many outside the Charnley camp who felt that Ray had an undue influence over Dave's career but you will not find any criticism from Dave himself. Ray had no formal position within the Charnley entourage but he could always be found in the background somewhere. There is no doubt that he always had Dave's interests at heart and was a loyal friend and advisor.

As a young lad approaching 17 years, it is worth recounting what this move up to London entailed. He was still working five days a week as an apprentice boilermaker. At 5.30pm on Monday, Wednesday and Friday evenings he would catch a Green Line bus to Lambeth from outside the factory. When he arrived, Ray would take him to a local cafe and then he'd get in early to the gym before the others arrived. Training would finish just before 10pm and Dave would then have to catch a late bus back to Dartford. On Tuesday and Thursday evenings at least he could go home for his tea. Then it would be off again to the J and E Halls boxing gym where he had been given permission to train on his own. On Sunday mornings Dave once again travelled into the Fitzroy Lodge for a further session. If all this was not enough, Dave would also get up by himself at around 5.30am and do his running from the house. The only early morning runs he missed was when the weather was too bad. For a while Dave enjoyed the company of his pal 'Tich' Allison, brother of footballer Malcolm Allison, on his journeys to the Fitzroy but after a while Tich's interest waned.

All of the travelling cost money, money that young Dave could hardly afford. But he never once considered asking for help. This was where Ray Bartlett once again assisted Dave. Every now and again he handed Dave five shillings for his travelling expenses. Dave never ever found out whether this money came from Fitzroy Lodge funds or out of Ray's own pocket, but he never forgot this generosity. Dave is in no doubt that over his time at the Fitzroy Lodge this money more than covered his outlay.

When he started at Lambeth, Dave's principal trainer was Freddie Hill, and true to the previous promise no attempt was made to alter his stance. Freddie was a stickler for physical fitness, but even he knew just by looking at the Charnley body shape that this would not be an issue as far as this fighter was concerned. The biggest difference Dave experienced between training at the Dartford club and the Fitzroy Lodge was the quality of the sparring, and this proved to be a huge benefit for him.

With Dave approaching his 17th birthday in October 1952,

this meant that he would become a senior boxer meaning that he could fight anyone of his own weight – there were no age limits any longer. This is the stage at which his early promise would be put to the test by experienced, fully grown adults. Would the distractions outside the boxing ring prove too much for the young Charnley as they had done for many prospects before and since?

CHAPTER 2

ABA Champion and Bronze Medal

Scotland's Dick McTaggart won the Olympic gold medal in 1956 taking also the Val Barker Trophy for being the best boxer. He won an Olympic bronze medal in 1960 and also competed at the 1964 games. Dick was five times the ABA champion in 1956, 1958, 1960, 1963 and 1965. In a total of 634 amateur contests he won 610. But at Wembley on the 23 April 1954 in the ABA featherweight final, he was knocked down four times and halted within 90 seconds of the first bell sounding. The boy who destroyed him was 18 year old Dave Charnley. This performance serves to highlight the fact that at that time young Dave was probably the most exciting amateur boxer in the country, if not the very best.

Amateur boxing in the London area enjoyed phenomenal popularity. There were club shows held every other week at large arenas, all of them sell-outs. Indeed the London Divisional Finals when held at the Royal Albert Hall had all 7,000 tickets sold out days in advance. It was really difficult for routine amateur boxing fans to get tickets for any show. During this period, Dave Charnley became the jewel in the London amateur crown over the space of 18 short months.

In modern times top level amateur boxers in this country could expect to undertake between 15 and 20 contests in any two year period. Dave Charnley engaged in 43 fights over that same time span. There are further marked differences between amateur boxing today and 60 years ago. In Charnley's days boxers did not wear headguards, and there were no computer scoring of fights. The significance of this is that modern day scoring tends to ignore body shots, causing the boxers to concentrate on blows which will register quick head punches. It can therefore be argued that amateur boxing in the 1950s was much more akin to the professional game than is currently the case. Perhaps the only difference in those days was simply the duration of the bout. In many ways amateur boxing was considered a necessary qualification process through which aspiring professionals had to pass.

Charnley commenced his senior amateur career on 11 November 1952 at Mile End when he outpointed H Farqhuar of Stepney. His next fight was a month later on a Toby Club show at the same venue. Charnley stopped Jim Culwick of the Times gym in the 1st round after putting him down for a third time for the full count. The following day he was due to fight at a Post Office show in St Martins-le-grand but when he arrived at the venue his opponent had failed to appear. The enraged Charnley was assuaged when a fight was arranged for the following evening. He then embarked on a three and a half hours bus journey to Chiswick where he fought Alf Drew. He lost this fight and perhaps learned a valuable lesson in patience. He ended the year with a points victory over W Norman of Brixton Youths at Eltham after knocking his opponent down three times.

1953 opened up at the Kings Hall in Hackney, where on 7 January he once again locked horns with Alf Drew. After a very tough contest Charnley avenged his previous defeat by the Eton Manor fighter.

On 22 January Dave had his first tournament success when he won a 9st novices competition at Manor Place Baths in Walworth. In the first contest of the evening he stopped M O'Connor of Sidmouth in the last round. In his second fight he beat Len Mills of the News Chronicle and Star club and in the final he beat the heavy punching T Haddon of Willesden.

On 2 February Charnley had a *home* game fighting on J and E Halls show at their clubhouse in Kingsfield Terrace, Dartford. This was a fund raising event for the Dartford and Crayford Unit of the Sea Cadets. His opponent was a local lad, R Hope, who bravely withstood the punishment until the referee intervened in the 2nd round.

Victories followed in February against W Hurley at Woolwich and Alan Stephens at Walworth, both on points. It was then on to the South East London Division championships which served as the first rung in the qualification process for London boxers to get to the ABA finals. On 9 March at Eltham Baths Charnley stopped A Terry of St Mary's, Chatham in the 1st round with a body shot and later in the evening knocked out W Norman of Brixton Youths in the 2nd. The following night he met the holder, Pat Dempster from the Woolwich Catholic club. The unfortunate Dempster was pummelled from pillar to post and was eventually disqualified for hitting low and using his head.

The London Division finals were held that year in the Empress Hall on the evening of 25 March. In the semi-final Charnley met Alf Drew for the third time in as many months.

With one win apiece, Charnley was delighted to edge home on points, and prepared eagerly to meet Percy Lewis of Oxford YMCA in the final. Lewis was the English National Champion, and had boxed for Britain at the 1952 Olympic games. Charnley opened well but by the second round Lewis's body shots seemed to be taking their toll. Charnley kept coming forward in the last round and only Lewis's experience allowed him to score with counter punches. At the end the decision went to Lewis, but he had been pushed hard in a fight which brought great applause from the large crowd. Dave received a nice silver plaque from the London ABA for his efforts.

A week later Charnley was back in the ring at Manor Place Baths to take on previous victim, Alan Stephens of the Caius club. Although giving away weight Dave was able to keep his attacking opponent at bay. In the 2nd Charnley had Stephens rocking and had him down for an eight count in the last before securing a comfortable victory.

At Manor Place Baths on 20 April, Charnley met Donald Steff from West Ham who was the Army Unit champion of the Royal Army Ordnance Corps. This resulted in another points victory.

On the 23 May, Dave was chosen to represented Hammersmith against Belgium in a Coronation Tournament, where he outpointed the Belgium champion, Bob Roger of Ghent. He received a silver statue of a boxer on a black marble plinth.

Charnley was now reaching a stage, where after only six months in the senior circuit, he had practically outgrown the normal club boxing circuit. His performance against Percy

Lewis had identified him as a real star in the making and there were very few London boxers who could live with him. His aggressive attacking style was winning over the fans and his obvious popularity would have been an embarrassment to his shy, slightly introverted character. Nevertheless he had good people around him. At the club he had Freddie Hill, and in particular Ray Bartlett, who would ensure he was matched sensibly; his father, and his brothers, William and Joe, were always on hand with their support.

His next outing on 4 June was for the London ABA against the RAF at Clapham Common. His opponent was Pat Duffell, a southpaw from Oxford. This was yet another victory and again a silver plaque was awarded. Just over a week later Dave travelled abroad for the first time in his life when he fought again for the London ABA against Amsterdam. This time he was matched with the Dutch champion, Jan van der Zee, and although he won the contest he sustained a cut eye from a head clash which prevented him fighting the Dutch army representative in Rotterdam the following evening. On this occasion a lovely silver wreath was taken home to adorn the family sideboard.

Amateur boxing entered its summer break, and although Dave kept on training as usual, Bartlett, Hill and Fitzroy Lodge secretary Ernie Stagg must have reflected on their rising stars' progress. In eight months he had engaged in 21 contests, winning 19. He had won a novice tournament, the South East London Division, and lost narrowly to Britain's last Olympic representative at the weight. He had fought twice for London, and defeated the champions of Belgium and Holland. The anticipation of the forthcoming season must have been almost palpable.

The 1953-54 season opened with a bang for Dave because he was selected to fight for the British amateur team against West Germany being a late choice owing to Percy Lewis turning professional. It started with an horrendous journey. The team got to Harwich without too much of a problem, but the ferry trip to Amsterdam caused everyone to suffer from seasickness, and to add insult to injury, when they arrived in Holland the connecting train to Frankfurt had already departed. After a wait of eight hours they eventually got on the move and when they arrived in the German city all they could do was get their heads down before the fights started.

Although the West German squad were too strong for their British counterparts, winning 7-2, Dave won his fight on 26 September against Hans Peter Mehling on points. Britain's only other winner was Bruce Wells, although Ron Barton boxed a *no contest* bout. Three days later the British team moved on to Fulda, near Cologne, where they fought an unofficial international against Hessia. This time Dave beat the West German champion, Ernst Schnaber. Dave had now beaten the champions of Belgium, Holland and West Germany.

Dave was back at the Royal Albert Hall on 10 October and celebrated his eighteenth birthday by representing London this time against Ireland. His opponent from Dublin, Tommy Butler, caught Dave with a body blow in the 2nd which caused him to wince in pain, but when Butler continued to duck below the waistline to avoid the Charnley attacks, the referee stepped in and brought the action to a close. Although billed as a

London v Ireland contest, the silver tankard gifted to the London boxers suggested that they actually fought a Dublin and Leinster select squad.

Charnley's next fight had two important factors which would be important in the future. He was again selected to represent Britain in an international, this time against the French at Wembley. There were problems even before the first fight had started when the Fench boxing officials complained about the scoring arrangements. They argued, successfully as it turned out, that as the referees were to be English, then two of the three ringside judges should be French. This caused embarrassment on at least one occasion during the evening when one of the French judges scored a contest as a draw which in those days was illegal! Dave's opponent on 28 October was Cherif Hamia. As a professional Hamia went on to win the French and European featherweight titles before losing to Hogan 'Kid' Bassey for the then vacant world title in 1957. Hamia started strongly and appeared to be ahead after two rounds. In the last however, Charnley took control and had Hamia in real trouble. The decision in favour of Hamia was met with boos and jeers from the crowd, and the disappointed Charnley sat in his corner and wept with frustration. This was the first important message from the fight – that it was not always a good idea to let the decision rest with the officials! But, perhaps equally important that night was the presence of Arthur Boggis at ringside. We will learn more about Boggis in the future, however he would later claim that this was the performance which first alerted him to Charnley's potential as a successful professional boxer.

On 1 November the unofficial British amateur boxing

ratings were produced which showed that at featherweight the number one position was vacant due to Percy Lewis leaving the unpaid ranks, but Dave was listed as the top contender. Among the others at the top of their divisions were Joe Erskine, Henry Cooper, Bruce Wells, Les Morgan and Dick Currie.

A shock was in store for Charnley in his next contest against Roger Baldwin of Sidmouth on a Toby club show at Mile End on 3 November. In the 2nd round Baldwin fired out a short left hook followed by a right hand which dropped Dave to his knees for a count of nine. Maybe Roger should not have done that, because shortly after, Charnley dropped him twice with vicious body shots bringing the referee's timely intervention. This was a precursor to a surprise defeat for Charnley eight days later at Manor Place Baths when he lost on points to Tommy Nicholls of Sankey's in Wellington. Perhaps Dave was suffering from too many strenuous contests in such a short period of time? His amateur club officials certainly thought so, because he was withdrawn from the London team to fight the Army on 1 December.

The Charnley family because of their staunch Scottish background, were looking forward to Dave's next fight on 12 December at the York Hall in Bethnal Green. He was now back to full fitness and ready to fight for a Repton select against a Scottish select. The organisers of the competition discovered that Dave's uncle, Jimmy Shaw, played the bagpipes and hired him to *pipe* the Scottish boxers into the ring. Uncle Jimmy only agreed when he was allowed to *pipe* Dave into the ring as well. His opponent was a new Scottish star, Bobby Neill. Neill fought out of the Sparta Amateur Boxing Club from Edinburgh, and although he had only eight contests, the Scottish boxing public had great hopes for him. This confidence was not misplaced and a perfectly timed right hand had Charnley down in the first round. But Dave was learning all the time, and when he got to his feet he boxed with more caution and picked up the pace in the 2nd and 3rd rounds to win the fight restoring his family's Anglo-Scottish pride.

Four days later, on a London Fire Brigade tournament at Bermondsey Baths, Dave took on Darlington's Northern Counties champion, Jim Leach. In the 2nd round Charnley forced Leach to the ropes and cut loose until the Northern lad dropped to the canvas. Although he was up quickly, the referee had seen enough, and despite Leach's protests, the fight was called off.

On New Years Day, 1954, Dave was in the ring again, this time back at J and E Halls clubhouse in Dartford. His opponent was Ron Jones who although a member of West Ham boxing club was, on this occasion, fighting for the Army. Jones was put down four times in the 2nd round and was stopped shortly after the start of the 3rd. After the fight Dave was presented by with a pair of gold cufflinks in recognition of the part he had played in putting local amateur boxing in Dartford on the map.

For months Dave and his family had been clamouring for a fight up in Scotland so that his relatives there could see in person what they had all been hearing about in telephone calls and letters. The Fitzroy Lodge club and Covent Garden then pulled resources and arranged such an event up in Glasgow for 26 January. Their plans were almost scuppered in the Fitzroy lodge gym when their 15st heavyweight, Brian Jelley, stood on Dave's foot causing severe bruising. A fight against J Reece at Hoxton was cancelled but his Scotland trip went ahead. The fights held at Milliken Park were attended by two busloads of Charnley supporters from Craigneuk accompanied by relatives from Dartford. The tournament ended in a 4 – 4 draw, with Dave winning his fight over T Ball who outweighed him by half a stone.

Charnley was on his travels once again on 5 February, this time to Berlin to fight for London against a local select. At the end of the match Berlin had won the competition 5-4, but in what was reported to be the best bout of the evening Dave beat Horst Stutz on a technical knockout in the 3rd round. The boxers all received an unusual silver disc inscribed 'BBV Box-stadenkampf, London v Berlin'.

In what could have been a preview of the forthcoming London Divisional finals, Dave took on Fred Woodman of Earlsfield on 22 February. Although never in danger Dave fought cautiously and there was little to separate them in the first two rounds. In the third the fight came alive with Woodman deciding at last to throw the right hand although this also galvanised Charnley who won the fight on points.

On 6 March Dave beat R Warnes of the Erith club in the 2nd round to start his defence of the South East London Division qualifiers and this sent Dave forward with renewed expectations for the battles ahead.

Dave only had one bout in order to win the South East title at Eltham on 8 March. His opponent Len Mills of the Lynn club was stopped with a cut eye in the 3rd round, but it was not all plain sailing. In the 1st round Mills effectively deployed the antidote for a southpaw, a succession of strong right crosses, and looked to have clinched the round. In the next round Charnley opened up and Mills got on his bicycle. In the last the referee had no alternative but to stop the fight due to the gash over Mills' eye.

The Charnley bandwagon moved on to the Royal Albert Hall for the London Divisional finals on 15 April. This is the point where his hopes of the ABA title fell the previous year following his defeat by Percy Lewis. Although Dave went on to win, the route to that success was not entirely satisfactory. Firstly opponent Fred Woodman was disqualified in the 2nd round, and in the final Alf Drew followed in similar fashion when he was thrown out in the 1st. Nevertheless, Dave was now through to the ABA finals at Wembley.

As usual the ABA finals were all held on the one evening, this time the 23 April. In Dave's featherweight division the other three semi-finalists were Bobby Drennan, the Scottish champion, Malcolm Collins, the Welsh champion, and Dick McTaggart from the RAF who was the Services champion. In his semi Dave outpointed Collins, while McTaggart had a similar win over his countryman. We have already noted McTaggart's future credentials both at home and abroad, and of course in 1954 very few could have predicted his staggering success in the unpaid ranks. Many experts of the amateur game will argue that Dick was our best ever and they could provide solid evidence to back this up. But on this night, in this arena, he had no chance. With his first punch, a left hook, Charnley dropped McTaggart for a count of six. Over the next minute or so Dick spent most of his time being knocked down and picking himself up before the referee decided he had seen enough. The Fitzroy Lodge had their first ever ABA champion. To this day Dave still retains the large silver cup presented to ABA winners during that era.

There is a humorous footnote to Dave's glory night. A bus load of friends and relatives from Craigneuk had travelled all the way down to London. As Scottish boxers including Dick Currie and John Smillie entered the ring they were met with vociferous cheers from the Lanarkshire contingent. But when *Englishman* Charnley stopped Scotsman Mc Taggart the same group burst into boisterous celebrations much to the confusion of other spectators. It took some time for the message to get across!

Charnley was back in action six days later when he underscored his ABA win with another 1st round knockout at Mile End over the hapless J Culwick. It was no surprise when the unofficial British amateur rankings were produced on 1 May and had Dave as the featherweight champion. The heavyweight champion was Brian London. Charnley's third, first round knockout in succession followed on 28 May when while representing Britain against the Imperial Services at the Royal Albert Hall, he stopped Ken Thomas.

At the Fitzroy Lodge annual dinner at Wingfield House, South Lambeth Road Dave was presented with a silver trophy and a pen and pencil set by Mr H G H Chandley the club's patron. Also that night came the announcement of the ill-health retiral of secretary Ernie Stagg who had fought hard during the war to keep the club alive.

It was now all systems go for the Empire Games to be held in Vancouver, Canada in August. To be entirely accurate the title of the Games had been changed in 1952 to the 'British Commonwealth and Empire Games' and a total of 24 countries would be represented. In these events, even up to the present day, the four Home Countries can send their own teams. This fact caused significant newspaper interest as far as the respective boxing teams were concerned. The England ABA kept delaying the announcement of their squad, primarily on financial grounds. They estimated that it would cost them £200 (roughly £5,000 today) for each member they sent. With the delay, the Scottish ABA saw an opportunity and contacted the secretary of the English ABA to advise them that they were considering selecting Dave due to his Scottish parentage. When the press got wind of this they contacted him and asked what his nationality was. Dave told them he was Scottish, and with that, off went a reporter to Somerset House to check the actual birth certificate. He of course discovered that Dave had been born in Dartford so he got in touch again with Dave and sought clarification pointing out that he had been born in England. Dave response was priceless. He said that he was still Scottish and added that if he had been born in a stable, it wouldn't mean he was a horse! When all this came out, the English selection committee quietly made it known to Dave that regardless of who else would be chosen, HE was certainly going with the English team! If a stranger were to ask Dave today what his nationality is he would be coy with his answer. This would be typical because he has a real fear of upsetting anyone. However, when the subject is raised by those close to him he simply points to his heart and says 'Scottish'.

Around this time Dave and his brother Joe were approached

by Ron Barton who had recently turned professional with manager Arthur Boggis. He had been sent by the *twins*, Reggie and Ronnie Kray to enquire with Charnley if he would be interested in meeting them. A few days later Dave travelled to a boxing gym above a pub in London and he met both Krays upstairs. They offered to handle his professional career, with a third person being put up as his manager, in name only. This person was thought to have been Alex Steene. Dave was given a week to consider matters. He returned at the appointed time and advised the Krays that he had decided to reject their offer. Dave says that they were absolute gentlemen and that they brought no pressure to bear on his decision.

On the 11 June the selectors finally announced the England team; Brian Harper (later known as Brian London), Bruce Wells, Nicky Gargano, Dave Charnley and George Whelan. The squad were due to fly out to Canada on the 19 July but beforehand they had to be kitted out in their nice navy blue blazers, white shirts, red, white and blue ties and grey flannels. Before departure they were accommodated at the Ecclestone Hotel in Victoria and their stay there was limited to press interviews and the occasional walk about the local streets.

On arrival in Vancouver after a long and tiring journey the team were housed in a school building which had a gym attached to it. The accommodation was quite satisfactory and Charnley had no problems settling in. His first fight of the Games paired him with the Australian representative Gilbert Durey on 1 August. Durey surprised Charnley in the 1st round when he pushed him to the floor, but Dave leaped to his feet and returned the compliment. Both tore into each other throwing hefty body shots but towards the end of the round Durey emerged from an exchange with a badly cut eye. The referee had no alternative but to award the fight to Charnley. This victory meant Dave was already assured a medal and he came out on the 5 August to fight South African Len Leisching with some confidence. However, Dave had to content himself with a bronze medal because his wily opponent threw his right hand constantly and deserved the points decision.

A humorous postscript to these Games was the indirect benefit they had for Dave's 14 year old brother Joe. When he returned home Dave gave his England blazer to his brother. One night Joe and a few of friends went up to London to see a film. When they arrived at the cinema there was a long queue but a sharp eyed usher spotted the blazer. Joe was approached and asked who he was. He made up a name and told the usher he had been in the England swimming squad, leading to himself and his pals being taken straight in to see the show, with the public wondering who the *star* was being taken in ahead of them!

By this time Dave had a steady girlfriend from Dartford, Ruth Vincent, and surprisingly for an 18 year old who was obsessed with training, she managed occasionally to persuade him to take her to the dancing. Shortly after his return to England Dave travelled to Scotland for a two week holiday with an uncle to show his Scottish relatives his medal. Dave felt he had gone as far as he could in the unpaid ranks and was keen to let his fists earn him some much needed cash. There were those in the ABA who were suggesting he should keep his vest for another two years and try his hand at the next Olympic Games, but this was never seriously considered. As soon as Dave had returned from Vancouver he had been contacted by Arthur Boggis who persuaded him to turn professional. It was in September 1954 that Dave took out his boxers licence, and the usual manager/boxer contract agreed.

CHAPTER 3

Learning and Earning

Arthur Boggis was not a particularly popular man. He had been a professional fighter in the 1930s and since then had been involved in all aspects of boxing including that of a trainer, corner man and then a manager. However outside the ring he was a butcher turned meat trader and had become reasonably wealthy owning property in Kensington. He had an arrogance about him which was often brought to the surface when he would openly criticise the quality of the meals he received in restaurants owned by friends, even though he was not expected to pay. Central London appeared to be like a magnet to him and whenever he travelled beyond these confines he seemed to be uncomfortable until he returned. He seldom, if ever, joined the after fight celebrations preferring to visit a friendly restauranteur for yet another *free* meal. He was not married but had a permanent companion, Madelaine, who was either Belgian or French.

When he became Dave's manager in 1954 he already had other fighters on his books, most notably the light-heavyweight mentioned previously, Ron Barton, but also Billy Hazelgrove, Tommy Barnham Jack Hobbs and Martin Thornton. Regardless of Boggis's apparent notoriety, what is not in doubt was his ability to spot fistic talent and to nurture that talent in an expert way. Until virtually the end of Charnley's career most people would agree that he did a good job. What was also not in doubt was the fact that throughout the time they worked together they both prospered financially and only towards the end of his career did Dave begin to closely question what Boggis was doing behind the scenes. Dave's brother, William, remembers him and Dave meeting Boggis for the first time. Neither brother, nor any of their immediate family, owned a car. In fact they had seldom even been in one. We can imagine the impression Boggis created in their young minds when he arrived in a new Humber Super Snipe, a top quality car of the period. He then drove them to his offices in central London but not before giving them the grand tour of his butcher shops. William recalls arriving at one of them, and Boggis pointing out one of his own vans being driven from the side of his shop. Boggis told the impressionable lads that he knew the driver was stealing meat from him. William and Dave began discussing how they would *corner* the driver and started to get out of Boggis's car. Boggis had to stop them and went on to explain that although the driver was taking meat from him, he also ran the most profitable shop, taking in more than £150 per week.

When Dave turned professional Boggis immediately had him enrolled at the famous Thomas à Beckett gym in the Old Kent Road, but surprisingly when viewed from the present time, he didn't have a proper trainer. Dave maintains he trained himself. He acknowledges that Boggis would offer advice, Ray Bartlett would organise sparring partners, Danny Holland, the manager of the Beckett, would help and Bill Chevally would assist particularly with massages. But in terms of deciding what exercises would be performed, in what volume, and when, Dave was his own master. It is worth recording that Danny Holland maintained a very clean and tidy gym which was no mean feat considering the volume of fighters using the facilities. The changing rooms were clean, the showers were in good condition and the equipment was always dried out and put away neatly. Dave can't recall paying a fee to use the gym, although Boggis may have taken care of this if it was required.

Contemporary sources claim that Boggis had very little skill in terms of coaching fighters which was surprising given his background. He seemed to have been fascinated by knockouts. When opponents were put forward by matchmakers for Dave, Boggis's first question was to ask if they had ever been knocked out and when he got excited in the corner his sole instruction to Dave was to scream 'Knock him out!'.

Sports historian Norman Giller, who provided the foreward for this biography, told me: 'When I was a young reporter on Boxing News, Arthur Boggis was a regular visitor to our Fleet Street office, usually picking the brains of Editor Tim Riley, records master Ron Olver and myself about any young amateurs worth signing. Between us, Tim, Ron and I knew everything there was to know in that era when amateur boxing was huge. I don't enjoy speaking ill of those no longer around to defend themselves, but let's say Arthur made himself very difficult to like. He was opinionated, and abrasive. I was looking at him through young eyes, and was unimpressed. Perhaps if I had been older and more worldly I might have judged him more kindly, but I have to confess he was not my cup of tea – or plate of chops, thinking of him in the context of his trade as a butcher'.

Dave soon had bought himself a small Hillman car to get him

from Dartford into London, and this allowed him greater flexibility regarding his training schedule.

In his first 14 months as a professional Dave engaged in 17 contests, against gradually improving opponents. In those days having an undefeated record was not critical, what was more important was the need to learn the rudiments of the game in order to build solid foundations. Different types of opposition were chosen. Tall, rangy boxers, fast boxers, big punching boxers, counter punchers, and skilful defensive fighters, all would be needed, not only to improve Charnley's skills, but to allow Boggis to gauge just how far his young protégé could go. Boggis wasn't about to waste his time and money on no-hopers!

Dave's first fight was on a Jack Solomons show at Harringay on 19 October 1954. Also scheduled to appear were Basil Kew, Terry Gooding and Henry Cooper. Around this time the 29 year old Ray Bartlett left the Fitzroy Lodge club due to a fall out with older members and the extra time he could now devote to Dave's career would not have went amiss.

The first opponent was Malcolm Ames of Croydon, who from 11 contests had won 5. The fight was stopped in the 3rd round by the referee after Ames had taken several counts. Boggis took his young star to a nightclub afterwards to celebrate. Young Dave was surprised and quite flattered when a blond female sat beside him and seemed to be chatting him up. However, she suddenly got up and left leaving Dave wondering if he had said something wrong. A short time later, Dave was even more surprised when the blond appeared on the stage and started her routine. Dave couldn't quite work out how Boggis and the others seemed to be enjoying the look on his face. The penny dropped when the blond was revealed as Danny La Rue!!

The fights were being arranged thick and fast. It was off to Blackpool Tower on 12 November for a second round knockout of Percy James from nearby Southport. Eleven days later and Dave was back at his old stomping ground at Manor Place Baths in Walworth where he had to travel the full six rounds before securing another victory over Roy Paine from Notting Hill. On this Stan Baker promotion, two other former ABA champions were on display, Henry Cooper and Freddie Reardon.

His final fight of the year should have been against Ronnie Neale of Bow, and in fact the programme for this Jack Solomons show at Harringay on 7 December listed Neale as the opponent. Indeed the programme notes indicated that Charnley had his call up for National Service deferred due to his continuing apprenticeship as a boilermaker. On fight night his opponent turned out to be Pat McCoy from Galway.

McCoy surprised Charnley by storming onto the offensive with arms flailing like windmills. Dave soon got to grips with the fight and was jabbing confidently. By the 6th round the referee had seen enough believing that McCoy was too far behind to win the fight. Mc Coy protested but the fans thought the decision was about right.

Historical Note – 1954
This was the year in which the BBC first broadcast their daily news programme on television.
Bill Halley recorded *Rock Around the Clock.*
Roger Bannister ran the first sub four minute mile, and Marilyn Munroe married Joe Di Maggio.

In 1955 Dave was to take part in 13 fights. Even in those days this was a huge undertaking for a young boxer. Boggis was obviously intent on bringing Charnley forward to championship level even though he would be banned from fighting for the British title until he had reached 21 years of age. With Dave's enthusiasm for training, and his apparent inability to relax even after a hard fight, there is no doubt he was up for the challenge. By the end of the year he would be fighting opponents who were rated highly in the unofficial British rankings in the lightweight division, and foreign boxers of note. Reports from the time clearly suggest that Dave was a very quiet and reserved young man. The following story demonstrates this very well. Still working as an apprentice boilermaker Dave used to drive his older brother William and a friend to work most mornings. After several months of this arrangement, William's friend happened to mention that he had realised after reading the morning paper that William's brother had received a cut eye the previous evening and wondered if it had been a bad one. William, perplexed, told him to look for himself. The puzzled friend was advised to look at the driver and only then did William realise that he didn't know this was Dave! Apparently sometime in the past, Dave had been pointed out across the factory floor as a professional boxer, and when the friend looked over he saw another workmate with facial injuries after falling from a bicycle. He thereafter simply assumed that this was Dave, and Dave hadn't made him any the wiser! Dave's supervisors at Vickers were obviously proud of their sporting hero and it became the norm that with each fight he would be granted three days off, the day before, the day of the fight and the day after.

It was off up to Blackpool Tower again for his first fight in the New Year against another Southport fighter, Andy Monahan. Boggis couldn't make this trip and Dave travelled with a trainer from the Thomas à Beckett, Benny Edwards. On the afternoon of the fight brother William and uncle Jimmy Shaw arrived at Dave's hotel. They were invited up to the room where they met Benny. Unaccustomed to the high life, the trainer ordered tea and toast for everyone, explaining that the hotel provided these refreshments free of charge. Sure enough these were delivered and no money exchanged hands. William and Jimmy were impressed.

Dave's fight was put on after the interval but before it started William noticed an argument between Benny and Dave. Nevertheless, Monahan stormed from his corner only to be neatly side stepped and met with crisp right hand counters. Left and right hooks to the body dropped the Southport lad and the fight was all over in 65 seconds. Afterwards William asked what all the fuss was about in the corner. Dave said that Benny kept instructing him to go out at the bell and keep throwing punches. Dave had eventually lost his patience and asked him 'what the bloody hell do you think I'm going to do?'. This was not the final row with the erstwhile assistant. On the hotel bill the following morning Dave discovered he had to pay for around 20 cups of tea and toast which ate into his £25 purse!

Almost three weeks later Dave was back in London at the Royal Albert Hall where again he made short work of Gold Coast fighter, Nye Ankrah, brother of Roy Ankrah who would later win the Empire featherweight title. Ankrah was met by a left hook to the body and a series of head shots forced him to the ropes. Three further body shots doubled the African over and a right to the chin jack-knifed him over the lower ropes drawing the referees intervention. These two wins would be

Charnley's quickest inside the distance victories for over six and a half years.

Next up for Dave was Neville Tetlow from Manchester at Harringay. Tetlow was no match for a rampant Charnley and he was floored for two long counts in the 1st round after heavy shots to the chin. Just after the 2nd round started another left from Charnley finished the job.

Following these three quick wins Boggis decided that a more solid test was required and they didn't come any tougher than Willie Lloyd from Crickhowell in Wales. Lloyd was a fully established lightweight but usually fought over that limit. Accordingly Boggis insisted on the match being made at 9st 10lb to ensure the weight differential in Lloyds favour was not too great. The fight was scheduled for Liverpool Stadium on 17 February. At the weigh-in on the day of the fight Lloyd weighed 1lb over the agreed limit, and even although he was six and a half pounds heavier than Charnley manager Boggis waived the usual forfeit. Lloyd at this time was the Welsh champion.

Dave started strongly against Lloyd who was a veteran of 28 fights and was six years older. Lloyd was taking punishment in the early stages and two hooks put him down for a count of nine. Charnley expended a lot of energy trying to finish him but the Welshman fought back fiercely and had Charnley down twice for short counts. After six rounds many at ringside had Lloyd in front, but Dave battled forward for the last two rounds to earn himself a creditable draw. Afterwards nobody was too despondent with the result because it was recognised that Lloyd was a significant step up, and someone who would have given all the top lightweights in the country a run for their money. Dave would fight Lloyd on a further two occasions.

Certainly Charnley should have learned of the need to pace himself a bit more after the Lloyd fight. It was obvious that his fast start and his eagerness to finish the stunned Welshman left him drained in the middle rounds and only his superb stamina saved him from defeat. At the Royal Albert Hall in March Dave met Denny Dawson from Sheffield and this lesson seemed to have escaped his notice for he launched into the Yorkshireman throwing dazzling combinations which thrilled his growing number of fans. Again the wily Dawson weathered this early storm and tried to force himself back into contention by throwing long right leads, the ideal foil for southpaws. However in the 7th round Dawson came in with his head down and everybody in the arena heard the subsequent clash. Dave was cut over the eye and the referee had no hesitation in disqualifying Dawson.

Dave needed time off to let his injured eye heal and he wasn't back in the ring for almost twelve weeks. Although no fights were scheduled his training regime never missed a beat. The only difference was that he missed a few weeks sparring and in this regard Dave was starting to earn himself an unenviable reputation among the fight fraternity. Generally speaking fighters didn't go flat out with sparring partners using the sessions to perfect techniques and improve on their ringcraft. This was not the case with Dave. He treated these sessions as real fights and didn't hold back. Of course both boxers would be wearing headguards and large gloves but nevertheless his punches still hurt. Many sparring partners came for one day and never returned, Steve Ellwood being one such person. On another occasion regular sparring partner George Martin was hired by Ray Bartlett. Apparently Martin had recently suffered a rib injury but neither Bartlett nor Dave had been aware beforehand. During sparring Dave dug in a body punch and George sank to the floor writhing in agony. Some of those watching complained to Bartlett but his attitude was that Martin had known what to expect and was being well paid.

One of Dave's regular sparring partners around this time was Bob Paget. Bob's view was that Charnley was perfectly entitled to spar as he did, how else could he prepare properly for his fights? Bob used to cycle to the Thomas à Beckett during his lunch hour for a few rounds with Dave, earning himself almost a week's wages in the process. Without being boastful he knew he could survive the Charnley attacks quite skilfully and keep the young star on his toes with counter punches. Bob realised early in his career that he would not become a champion in the professional ranks, so decided to earn as much as he could by sparring almost anyone available. It is alleged that he even went into the ring with Henry Cooper! Bob argues with great logic that by being a sparring partner he did not need to pay a manager or a trainer, and being paid in cash meant that the taxman didn't know too much about it.

Dave returned on the 24 May back at the Royal Albert Hall and once again he won by disqualification. His opponent this time was Jeff Walters from Scarborough and it was a thrilling slugfest. Within the first minute of the contest Charnley had Walters down twice, but Walters came back and put Dave down near the end of the round. In the 2nd, following a combination of left and right hooks to the chin Charnley had Walters down for a count of nine. The fight settled down for a spell until the 6th when Walters deliberately butted his opponent and was immediately thrown out by the referee.

A fortnight later Dave travelled back into his opponents back yard this time to Birmingham. Facing him was 68 fight veteran Johnny Mann. Mann had won 43 of the fights and was considered to be just short of championship class. Again Boggis was choosing Dave's opposition wisely, gradually stepping up the quality and looking to get more competitive rounds under his belt. This turned out to be a keenly fought contest with the local man giving everything he had. Mann was badly cut over an eye in the 4th and in the next round was staggered by a left hook. Every time it looked as if Mann would succumb he fought back bravely with right crosses and left hooks. However he simply didn't have the strength to hold off his young foe, and lost decisively on points.

Arthur Boggis must have made friends in Birmingham, because towards the end of July, he had Dave back up there to fight Cardiff boxer, Teddy Best. In a fight scheduled for eight rounds, Charnley once again dominated proceedings from beginning to end, with Best lucky to last the distance. Charnley was still struggling with pacing himself however, and although he knocked Best from pillar to post for the first three rounds he began to tire. Best rallied in the 4th and 5th and made the fight interesting. This brief respite did not last long however, and as Charnley gathered his second wind the Welsh boxer was cut over the left eye and then felled for a long count in the 6th. The brave

Best refused to surrender and hung on grimly over the last two rounds to see out the fight.

Dave had now earned himself a two months break from competition, but his mentality for hard training did not allow him to rest his body from the rigours of roadwork and exercising in the gym. All through his career this work ethic never waned. There is no doubt Dave saw his boxing career as a job. A job he wanted to be successful in and this ambition drove him to be as fit as he possibly could at all times. No distractions were allowed. After his fights Dave would go straight home and soak in a hot bath. He says that he didn't feel pain from the punches he absorbed, but his muscles ached from the exertions. He sometimes felt that this happened due to the tension he experienced before his fights started. The day after his fights he would visit the gym and get a massage from Bill Chevally and only then would the muscle aches start to dissipate. Around four days after the contests, Dave would be back in light training and this regime never altered for the duration of his career, even when it reached its peak.

Between his fight with Best, and the end of 1955, the quality of Charnley's opposition took a decidedly upward turn. Over the next two months he would face three fighters rated in the British top ten, a top quality foreign opponent and an experienced journeyman, just for good measure.

His first challenge in this demanding programme was against Stan Skinkiss up in Nottingham on 3 October. Skinkiss had had 44 fights and that year alone had fought both Willie Lloyd and Johnny Mann among others. In 1952 he had taken Hogan 'Kid' Bassey into the 7th round, and Bassey would later go on to win the World featherweight title. He was ranked number seven in Britain. The Mancunian never knew what hit him. He was down for a count of six in the 1st round and a further twice in the 3rd. Early in the 4th a Charnley punch opened up a severe gash on Skinkiss's lower lip and the referee saw this as an ideal opportunity to halt proceedings. Charnley, less than a year in the professional ranks, had burst into the British top ten.

Ten days later and he was delighted to be back in the ring at the Royal Albert Hall on a Harry Levene promotion to face Preston's Jackie Butler rated number ten in Britain. Dave continued where he had left off with a thumping victory. He hammered Butler from start to finish, and the Preston man's only means of defence was to continually clinch. In the 4th he finally went down for a long count, and on rising he was immediately put under so much pressure that the referee Harry Bentley had to come to his rescue.

Just over two weeks later another top ten fighter, Leo Molloy from Birkenhead, stepped up to the plate at Earls Court. Molloy was a good cagey fighter who knew his way around a boxing ring. He was a different type of foe than either Skinkiss or Butler, and would pose Charnley different problems with his good ring movement and right crosses. Charnley was learning how to use his right jab, and his hook off this jab, and not to rely solely on his powerful swings. Molloy took a brief tumble through the ropes in the 5th round taking a short count but other than this he was never really in danger of being stopped, leaving Dave to win clearly on points. Dave's popularity was becoming obvious when six bus loads of fans travelled up from Dartford to London for the fight.

His next opponent was Frenchman Guy Gracia. Gracia was perhaps a step too far for the 20 year old at this stage, a rare misjudgement by Boggis. He had previously fought 41 times in France, Italy and Canada winning 29 of these. He had never been beaten inside the distance and two months previously he had lost on points over ten rounds to the current British champion, Frank Johnson.

At the end of the fight Charnley was distraught at having been outpointed over the ten rounds but his loyal fans weren't, as they cheered him from the ring. Charnley stood toe to toe with his 32 year old opponent without backing down. The fight didn't start well though for Dave because he was floored from a body shot in the 1st. Gracia covered up well when Charnley attacked and he countered accurately. Charnley had more success when he pinned the Frenchman to the ropes and let fly, but when the punches stopped, Garcia fired back stinging Dave repeatedly. The outcome was not a disaster, but it demonstrated to Dave and his team that he was not yet the full package.

In late November the trade paper, Boxing News, ran a poll of readers asking them to decide who was Britain's best prospect. Number one was Ron Barton, second was Peter Waterman, third was Dave Charnley, fourth was Dick Richardson and fifth was Brian London. It should be remembered that boxing was huge at this time with 250,000 people reading this paper every week. All the national newspapers had designated boxing reporters and with the advent of television these would be considered the golden years for the sport.

Dave's last fight of the year was at Nottingham on 28 November against Kurt Ernest of Exeter. The referee stopped the fight at the end of the 6th when Ernest's left eye was completely closed. Charnley was back to his brilliant best although Ernest gave as good as he got in the 4th and 5th and had the fans on their feet cheering both fighters. The only down side for Charnley was that he was cut over the right eye.

Soon after the fight was over the press were reporting that Charnley was to face Johnny Butterworth on 13 December as an eliminating contest for the British title, even though that at 20 years of age he would be ineligible to challenge for it until the following October. The bout was to be televised but Dave was withdrawn and instead Butterworth fought top notch Frenchman Lahouari Godih, losing badly.

Charnley had made considerable progress this year and had taken himself into contention for the British title. He showed he was now able to undertake the ten round distance without too much difficulty although he still seemed to rush things at the start. There was no doubting his punching ability to either head or body, although he had suffered a few cuts around the eyes. At the start of the year he was earning around £25 a fight and at the end his purses had risen to between £250 and £500. As the Boxing News poll showed he was one of Britain's rising stars for 1956.

Historical Note – 1955
America announces plans to arm intercontinental ballistic missiles with nuclear warheads
West Germany joins NATO
Dwight D Eisenhower is the US President
Winston Churchill resigns as Prime Minister to be replaced by Anthony Eden
Einstein dies in New Jersey
The polio vaccine is introduced

CHAPTER 4

British Title Contention and Married Life

1956 was to be a year of change for Dave, both in his career, and, perhaps more importantly, on the domestic front. It was a year in which he would move into contention for the British title, change training locations, became a major draw at the Box Office and marry his childhood sweetheart.

As the year opened up the Boxing News published their British rankings. The lightweight champion was still Frank Johnson with his challengers listed as Gordon Goodman, Joe Lucy, Johnny Butterworth, Johnny Miller, Sammy McCarthy, Dave Charnley, Stan Skinkiss, Paddy Graham, Leo Molloy and Jackie Butler.

Dave's first fight of the year was on a Morrie Jaye promoted show on 6 March at the Seymour Hall, Marleybone with him topping the bill against Rochdale's Johnny Butterworth in a contest carried over from 13 December. Butterworth had mixed in top level company. He had lost narrowly to Frank Johnson for the Central Area title, he had beaten Joe Lucy and drawn with Johnny Miller. Although not officially an eliminator for the British title, in most people's minds the loser would tumble back down the queue of fighters waiting to challenge Johnson. The referee was Pat Floyd. Charnley started quickly as usual and almost floored Butterworth in the 1st with a right hand. In the 2nd two rights to the head and a left to the body did the trick with Butterworth taking a count of seven. In the 4th the onslaught continued with Butterworth taking two further counts. In the next round it was clear Butterworth had no chance of lasting the distance and when a flurry of punches put him over the referee made a timely intervention bringing proceedings to an end.

After the fight, Dave told friends that Butterworth had landed a good right hand punch on his chin in the 1st round which had very little effect. Dave immediately sensed that his opponent had lost heart through this, and knew then that he'd win the fight.

Next up was Sammy McCarthy a great crowd favourite in London who carried a big following. He'd won 40 of 46 fights and had been British Featherweight champion. McCarthy had taken both Hogan 'Kid' Bassey (future World Featherweight Champion) and Ray Famechon (former European Featherweight Champion) the full distance before losing on points. He had also fought and lost in a challenge himself for the European title.

Following the victory over Butterworth Charnley was now a top flight attraction and Harry Levene was on a winner when he promoted the battle between the pair at the Royal Albert Hall on 3 April. Beforehand the respective camps had agreed a side bet of £500 for the winner and the bookmakers had McCarthy a 6-4 favourite. The venue was sold out weeks in advance and Dave had supporters travelling from all over the Dartford area. No one knew how many busloads in total had made the journey but it seemed like the numbers associated with football matches.

The Royal Albert Hall in Kensington is a unique venue for a boxing match. It is circular in design with towering red brickwork making it an imposing building. Once inside it seems like the arena was actually built for boxing. The ring sits neatly in the middle of the floor area surrounded by temporary seating. At the sides, steep circular rows extend upwards towards the roof, interspersed with private boxes. The high dome shaped roof adds to the excellent acoustics. The noise created by around 7,000 fervent boxing fans that evening was electrifying.

The fight got off to an exciting start with Mc Carthy going down in the 2nd from a left hook to the chin. In the 3rd Charnley was warned twice for low blows by referee Mick Fox before he took Mc Carthy down again from a right hook to the solar plexus. After this Charnley began to suffer from his usual mid-fight energy gap and Mc Carthy made up ground. In the 6th Dave was warned again for a low blow. In the 9th Mc Carthy slipped down for a final time possibly out of exhaustion as both fighters battled on encouraged by the huge roars from their supporters. As the final bell chimed referee Fox raised Charnley's arm without hesitation sparking sporadic outbursts of fighting between rival fans. This was a huge victory for Charnley and should have catapulted him into the number one contender status even though he was some six months short of his 21st birthday. It was therefore surprising that the loser went forward to challenge the new lightweight champion Joe Lucy two months later with the British title at stake.

Sammy McCarthy shared his memories about the fight. He recalls that prior to that contest he had been stunned in previous

1

3

2

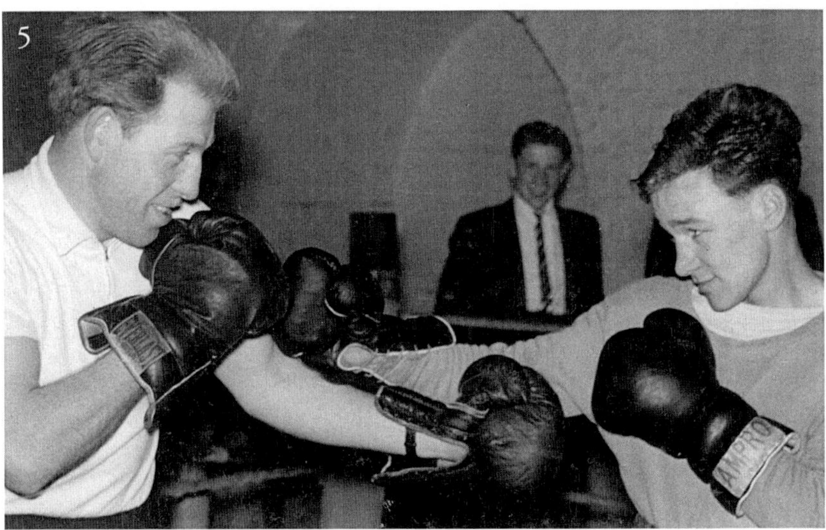

Previous page: 1: Grandfather David Fraser, with *curly top* Dave resting on the dog. *2:* Dartford and District ABC with Dave standing at the far right side. *3:* The young professional fighter. *This page: 4:* Dave is kneeling on the right with the rest of the British team who fought West Germany in Fulda on 29 September 1953. *5:* At the Fitzroy Lodge with principal coach, Freddie Hill. *Opposite page: 6:* Winning the British lightweight title from Joe Lucy. Arthur Boggis is on the left.

7: Dave and Peter Waterman land simultaneously *(courtesy of Derek Rowe). 8:* Corporal Charnley, Captain Hunter and three others on National Service.

contests following punches to the head which had left him groggy. However these never really hurt him as such. The only time during his career when he was really *physically hurt* was from Dave's right hook to the body in the 3rd round. Sammy says that when the punch landed he didn't feel anything but within a split second the pain hit him and he dropped to his knees in agony. He was in such discomfort he felt like crying. The fact that Sammy was able to continue for another seven rounds demonstrates remarkable courage and an extremely high level of fitness but also provides an example of the punching power of the Dartford man.

After Dave had showered and got his wounds attended to he made a point of going out to all the buses parked around the Albert Hall to thank his fans for their support a gesture which was greatly appreciated even to this day. As a coincidental anecdote to this fight, Dave's brother Joe, many years later, was performing jury duty at the Old Bailey when into the witness box to give evidence strode Sammy McCarthy!

It was around this time, perhaps with his earnings from the McCarthy fight, that Dave took his first step into the business world when he decided to buy a public house in Dartford. Considering the position his family were in during 1940, some sixteen years later he chose an apt name for the new enterprise – *Who'd have thought it?* With all Dave's commitments he assigned the management of the pub to his older brother William and his wife. Running a pub would not have been entirely alien to the Charnley family because Uncle Sam, when he retired from football, opened a pub in nearby Stone, which he called the *Lads of the Village.*

Dave was out of the ring for two and a half months after this, and when he returned on 19 June it was at Clapton Stadium against his second foreign opponent, Fernand Coppens, the Belgium champion. Dave weighed in at a career heaviest at that stage of 9st 10lb establishing himself as a fully grown lightweight. Surprisingly for Charnley who was usually quick out of the blocks, Coppens took the 1st round, impressing everyone with an uppercut and a succession of jabs. His joy was short lived however because he was knocked to the ground in the 2nd from a right hand and had to take an eight count. Coppens went down a further three times, and with the crowd baying for the fight to be stopped, the referee stepped in and ended the massacre.

Before his next fight the World lightweight rankings were released showing that Wallace 'Bud' Smith was the champion, followed by Larry Boardman, Duilio Loi, Jimmy Carter, LC Morgan, Ludwig Lightburn, Ralph Dupas, Cisco Andrade, Frankie Ryff, Johnny Gonsalves and Joe Brown. Dave would fight three of these fighters in the future and beat all of them inside the distance.

With all the travelling the Dartford fans had to undertake it was a pleasant surprise when Morrie Jaye announced that Dave's next fight would be held in the open air at the home of Dartford Football Club. His opponent was Johnny Miller from North Shields and his manager Jim Turner, upset at how Charnley was being touted as the next challenger to Joe Lucy, had been trying for some time to set up the match. For this fight Dave was training at a new gym, the Green Man in Blackheath. Ray Bartlett had been struggling to find sparring partners perhaps due to the distance the gym was away from central London. This didn't stop Bob Paget however who simply had to cycle a bit further from his place of work. Also now sparring with him was former victim Pat McCoy but he was still struggling for help however and Boggis had to advertise for others to join Paget and McCoy.

On 24 July around 4,000 fans turned up at the stadium to cheer on their local hero. The matchmaker for this fight was Jack Carey and the referee was Jack Hart. The northerner's hopes were soon dashed when he was put down for a long count near the end of the 3rd and indeed may have been saved by the bell. In the 6th he was floored by a left cross and when he got to his feet a glancing right put him down again. The referee was summoned by Jim Turner and the bout was concluded. It was announced later that Dave's purse for this fight was £1,000, not bad for a £6 per week apprentice boilermaker!

On 10 August the Boxing News published their unofficial British rankings and the champion was Joe Lucy followed by Dave Charnley, Sammy McCarthy, Johnny Miller, Johnny Mann, Gordon Goodman, Johnny Butterworth, Paddy Graham, Leo Molloy, Stan Skinkiss and Ron Hinson. Isn't it surprising when looked at from a modern perspective that Dave had already beaten six of those listed?

In the lead up to Dave's next fight all was not well. He was scheduled to fight on 27 August at the Maindy Stadium in Cardiff against old foe, Willie Lloyd. His fight was not top of the bill because the British heavyweight title contest between Joe Erskine and Johnny Williams was the main attraction. However this was still a major contest and there were many influential people who believed that Dave should not fight for the British title until he had beaten Lloyd, given that the Welshman had held him to a draw previously.

Boxers are like the rest of us in that they catch viruses and suffer illness just like everybody else. Very few footballers go through an entire season without missing matches for one reason or another. However there is a uniqueness with top level boxers particularly when they are like Dave Charnley, who by this time was topping the bill with almost every fight. What happens to a promotion if the star attraction falls ill and can't fight? Does the bill go ahead even though the fighter the fans all want to see will not be there? If the show is cancelled who pays all the bills connected with hiring the hall, ring, stewards and the printing of tickets?

Bob Paget recalls the situation clearly. Bob knew that Dave was stronger and quicker than himself but he could block, parry and fiddle his way around, clinching when necessary allowing himself to last the required distance during their sparring sessions. In the week leading up to the Lloyd fight, Bob knew something was amiss. Dave was weak and Bob was more than holding his own. On one occasion, in mid round, Dave suddenly stopped fighting, jumped out the ring and headed for the toilet. Bob, shocked, followed. When he got there Dave was hanging over a sink gasping for breath. Bob then approached Ray Bartlett who was in the gym and told him that there was something wrong and he shouldn't be fighting in Cardiff. Ray immediately phoned Boggis and told him what Bob had said. After Bob had got changed and was about to leave the gym Boggis phoned back and spoke to him. He told Bob in no uncertain terms that as manager he would decide if Charnley could fight and that it was none of Bob's business. Not surprisingly perhaps, Bob was never used as Dave's sparring partner again. Dave's brother William also has memories about the build up to this fight. About a week beforehand he met Dave and saw that he had sores around his mouth and appeared to be suffering from a heavy cold. At that stage William advised Dave to call the fight off but Dave refused telling him that his purse was £400. This was a huge sum for a 20 year old boilermaker's apprentice. Over the next few days Dave scrapped the sores off his mouth, and kept training. William regretfully admits that both he and Dave were desperate for the fight to go ahead because the money on offer to them at that time seemed an incredible amount.

On the night of this open air event the rain came tumbling down and before the Charnley-Lloyd contest the ring canvas had to be swept with brushes to remove the puddles. Both fighters had trouble keeping their balance at times and in the 3rd round Dave touched down following a stumble but the referee administered a count anyway. Later in this round Lloyd did put Charnley down with a right hand. By the 4th round Charnley's face was covered in blood and the fans knew a shock result was on the cards. By the last two rounds both fighters were struggling and had clearly ran out of steam. Referee Ike Powell raised the Welshman's hand at the end to great cheers from the locals. The fans were so pleased with the efforts both boxers had shown that *nobbins* were thrown into the ring. *Nobbins* was the traditional name given to the coins fans threw into the ring for the boxers when they thought they had witnessed an exceptional fight.

While Dave's previous defeat to Gracia was accepted as nothing more than a *learning experience* this result was different. There was a belief held by many within the British Boxing Board of Control that a fighter shouldn't challenge for the British title if previously beaten by another contender, although Sammy McCarthy's fight with Joe Lucy seemed to mitigate against this. Boggis's plans must surely have been to match Dave with Joe Lucy around his 21st birthday in October but this now seemed a forlorn hope.

There was much more serious news however for all concerned. The day after the fight Dave visited a man he knew as Captain Jack Moffat. Moffat and his business partner, Walter Freer, owned three greyhound tracks including the one in Crayford. Both men, much older than Dave, had befriended him, taken him under their wing, and were beginning to offer advice in terms of what to do with the money he was now earning. Moffat was concerned about how Dave looked, so much so in fact that he refused to let him leave his home, and sent for a car to take him to the St. John's and St. Elizabeth's Hospital in St. Johns Wood, London. When examined the doctors discovered that he had contracted pneumonia and was placed in a side room of his own. Dave's brother Joe claims that he was so unwell that his life was in danger and the family visited the hospital each day. Dave recalls that when he began recovering his senses he had no idea where he was. As was usual in those days for patients suffering from this type of illness, hospital staff would continually boil a kettle in a ward to create steam, thereby allowing the patient to breath more easily. So when Dave was coming to, in this misty environment, he saw a nun appearing at his bedside, and for a brief moment he honestly thought he'd died and went to heaven! Of course the nurses in this hospital were all nuns.

Of significance to Dave's future, although he wasn't to realise it at the time, was the result of the World lightweight title fight held in New Orleans three days before his fight with Lloyd, when Joe Brown beat the champion Wallace Smith on a majority decision.

By early November Dave was back in training at the Green Man, and he had been joined by Welsh heavyweight Dick Richardson who was preparing for his fight with world rated Nino Valdes. Dave had been told he would be fighting Belfast man, Al Sharpe, on the 16th in Manchester, but Sharpe opted out after losing recently to Boswell St Louis.

Dave eventually did get back into ring action at Manchester on that date against South African Alby Tissong. He was clearly not back to his best and looked lethargic for the first few rounds preferring to take his time and pick shots rather than going for broke. By the 6th however he had began to find the range and Tissong was lucky to hear the final bell. This was another clear points win.

With his fighting over for the year Dave could at last concentrate on his domestic arrangements, which would have been exactly what his fiancée Ruth had hoped for. The young couple were married on 8 December at the Holy Trinity church in Dartford where hundreds turned up to watch. Best man at the wedding was Dave's brother Joe and the reception was held at Stone Drill Hall. The young couple set up home in a nice mauve painted house in Thanet Road, Bexley. Ruth turned out to be a great supporter of Dave's boxing career and was at ringside for many of his fights. She once alleged to other friends' wifes that when Dave was watching his weight in preparation for upcoming fights, she would go on a diet with him.

By the year's end, with Joe Lucy as the British champion, Dave was unofficially ranked as the number one contender, with Willie Lloyd at number four. Speculation was now mounting that Dave would fight Willie Lloyd at the start of 1957 with Guy Gracia meeting Sammy McCarthy on the same bill both fights being promoted by Harry Levene.

It had been a mixed year for Dave. Following his important victory over leading contender, Butterworth, he had won the *Battle of London* with Sammy McCarthy before tripping over Lloyd. His serious illness had temporarily halted his strict training regime and the defeat from Lloyd had stalled his progress.

Historical Note – 1956
Olympic Games held in Italy
House of Lords defeats the bill to abolish the death penalty
Burgess and McLean re-surface in Russia
Elvis Presley has his first hit with *Heartbreak Hotel*
The Russians invade Hungary

CHAPTER 5

British Champion and National Service

The routine nature of Dave's life was to change considerably during 1957. He would eventually end his apprenticeship as a boilermaker and commence National Service duties. He put his finances on a more formal footing and through the fact that his fights would now be shown to a growing audience of television owners he would reluctantly gain celebrity status. His first fight of the new year was with someone he knew well.

Former opponent Welshman Willie Lloyd was not a bad guy. He was a tough lad and could handle himself in a boxing ring, however, Dave's upcoming fight with him on 22 January was starting to take on the status of a grudge match. While his fans were determined to see their man wipe the floor with an opponent who had drawn and beaten Dave in two previous meetings, Charnley himself, as always, saw the whole event as just another step on the ladder to future riches.

6,000 excited fans filled the Royal Albert Hall for this twelve round official elimination contest for the British title. Moreover, the fight would be seen by a far larger audience via television the following evening with Dave fighting on this new means of domestic entertainment for the first time.

The booing for Lloyd started in the 6th round when Charnley emerged from a clinch with a cut over his eye where Lloyd's head had caught him. In the following round a sweeping low blow from Lloyd lifted Charnley off his feet and over onto his back writhing in pain. Lloyd was to pay for these indiscretions however, because they roused a partially sleeping tiger, and a bitter Charnley went to town. Dave would uncharacteristically admit afterwards that he had never been as angry with an opponent.

Lloyd received a final warning from the referee in the 10th for butting and more boos rang out. Charnley tore into Lloyd and had him swaying from hooks leaving him struggling to stand. In the next round Lloyd took another hammering but there were still fears that Dave's eye injury would worsen. In the last round Lloyd eventually sank exhausted to his knees for a count of eight. When he got to his feet Charnley was on him in a flash and referee Bill Williams stepped in to stop the fight with 45 seconds to go in the last round, providing Charnley with the victory he craved. During the final round the six thousand fans were on their feet waving programmes, stamping their feet and cheering their hero to the roof of this famous old venue, with Lloyd the unfortunate villain of the piece.

Most ringside observers felt that Lloyd had won only two of the rounds and was well beaten at the finish. When the referee stopped the fight, as a gesture of satisfaction, Dave spat out his gumshield and kicked it out the ring. Some time afterwards journalist Reg Gutteridge would take a copy of the fight to Pentonville Prison and the prisoners stood and cheered when they saw Dave's reaction.

That same night saw Guy Gracia continue to haunt the British lightweight scene by beating Sammy McCarthy.

On 13 February lightweight champion of the world, Joe

Brown, made his first defence of the title in a return match with the man he took it from, Wallace Smith. The fight this time was held at Miami Beach, Florida with Smith retiring on his stool at the end of the 10th round.

Meanwhile back in Britain the big fight on the horizon was the British lightweight contest between the champion, Joe Lucy, and his new challenger Dave Charnley. The right to promote the contest was won by Jack Solomons and it was scheduled for 9 April at Harringay Arena in north London. From the minute the fight was announced the anticipation amongst the fans of both boxers was intense. There was plenty of side issues for the media to get their teeth into one example being the fact that they were southpaws. In addition both were publicans. Lucy, originally from Mile End, was the manager of the famous Thomas à Beckett while Dave still owned the *Who'd have thought it?* in Dartford. It was fortunate that Dave had changed his training quarters to the Green Man from the Beckett thus saving any potential embarrassment, but as it turned out Lucy set up camp at the Star and Garter pub in Windsor.

Once again Dave was struggling to find suitable sparring partners, and probably as a gimmick Boggis actually claimed to have sought permission to use the new Olympic champion, Dick McTaggart. Tickets went like hot cakes and ranged from 10 shillings to £5 guineas. Contemporary records suggest that Dave sold over 2,000 tickets to his fans in and around Dartford, and local newspapers reported that on the night 50 buses left Dartford for Harringay.

A few days before the fight Courage and Barclay, the brewing firms, organised a boxing luncheon at the Noah's Ark public house situated near the old Blackfriars ring in Blackfriars Road. Joe Lucy's Thomas à Beckett sold Barclay ales, while Dave's *Who'd have thought it?* was a Courage pub. Neither boxer could attend due to the advanced stages of their training, but promoter Jack Solomons was delighted with the *free* publicity anyway.

Before this fight brother Joe moved into the Charnley family home in Thanet Road, a routine which would continue in the future, especially prior to championship contests. This provided Dave with an extra distraction from the fight as the nerves started to build and gave him someone to talk with during the car journey into training. It also became a habit that on the morning of the weigh-in, Dave and Joe would walk to and from Crayford greyhound stadium from Bexley to *test* weigh Dave on Captain Moffat's giant scales.

The weigh-in on the day of the fight was held at Solomons gym in Windmill Street, near Piccadilly, and there was a surprise when Lucy had trouble making the 9st 9lb limit. This usually indicates that a fighter has had to starve and dehydrate himself which in some cases has a detrimental effect on his ability to stay strong in the latter stages of the fight.

The contest started as a bit of a maul but Lucy with his nice jabs appeared to be slightly ahead after four rounds. By the 5th the fight had become untidy and in that round and the following one both boxers fell to the canvas twice and were warned by referee Andy Smyth. The Harringay ring was bigger than most and this appeared to be favouring the light footed Lucy. However, in the 7th Charnley began to land with his hooks and the fight seemed to be turning his way. Lucy was in trouble for the first time in the 9th when hooks to the body and two rights to the chin troubled him. Worse was to follow for the champion when Lucy received a cut eye in the 11th.

Neutral observers had not been impressed with the quality on offer at this stage but the atmosphere changed just as the 11th drew to a close when Charnley was cut over his right eye. Right at the start of the 12th, Charnley moved onto the offensive catching Lucy often and putting him down twice for counts of eight each time. It seemed as if weight making was finally taking its toll on Lucy because he was tiring fast. In the 13th the champion was floored for a third time and the end looked in sight. The 14th opened with Dave's fans on their feet roaring their man on. Once again, in this round, Lucy was knocked down for a 4th time and it was a credit to his courage that he kept going when all seemed lost. In the last round both boxers were clearly almost out on their feet but Dave still managed to put Lucy down for a fifth time from body shots. At the end the referee's decision was a formality and the British title had changed hands.

Afterwards Lucy's manager Jim Wicks, who also managed Henry Cooper, said that his fighter would in future fight at a higher weight division, but in actual fact this didn't happen as Joe never fought again. He would not be the last boxer to retire after a thumping defeat from Charnley.

As a result of the title win a civic reception was held in Dave's honour at the Hesketh Park cricket pavilion. Dave's newly won Lonsdale belt sat on the main table in front of the Mayor, Councillor Huggett, who opened proceedings. Alderman Bareham and a neighbour of Dave's, Councillor Lenderyou also spoke before Councillor Mason reviewed his boxing career up to that date. There was also another surprise speaker in the shape of Charlie Selby who was Dave's *other* trainer in his role as an apprentice boilermaker at Vickers. Charlie told the hundreds in attendance that they had been workmates for the previous six years in the plater's shop. Also with Dave on this auspicious occasion was wife Ruth, his father William, his step-mother and other family members. Needless to say Dave would not agree to speak in response, claiming that he would rather get battered for fifteen rounds than undertake that task. He did however personally shake the hands of every single person at the reception.

Just prior to the Lucy fight, Dave had heeded the advice of his two unofficial mentors, Captain Jack Moffat and Walter Freer. They suggested he should engage the services of an accountant to look after his affairs. This he did and it was recommended that Dave should register himself as a limited company. Of course the newspapers got hold of the story and for the next year or so, particularly Reg Gutteridge, would refer to him as David Charnley Limited. It is of interest to know that Dave's purse for this fight was £1,000 and because it was broadcast by the BBC he had an additional income of £149.12s.6d. Out of this he had to pay tax to the British Boxing Board of Control of £40, £96 to sparring partners, £45 to his trainer, £3 to Bill Chevally for his massages, £6.7s.6d to his cornermen and £239.16s.0d to Arthur Boggis. He was granted £78 worth of tickets for his family and friends by the promoter and his £32 training fees at the Green Man were also paid. This left Dave with £700 in the bank and £19 in cash.

Dave's career was now being pushed forward at great pace. Chief promoter Jack Solomons and manager Arthur Boggis obviously thought that they had a future world champion on their hands and were determined to move him into world title contention. The first stage in this process was to match him with world ranked Johnny Gonsalves from Oakland, California.

Gonsalves occupied 9th position in the world ratings and had beaten former champions Wallace Smith and Paddy DeMarco. He was a former American amateur champion and had fought professionally on over 60 occasions. He was considered a very skilful boxer but had few stoppage victories although he had only been stopped twice himself.

On 4 June, again at Harringay, Charnley sampled world class boxing for the first time. Gonsalves was much taller than Charnley and had a long reach advantage. However, instead of electing to box at range, Gonsalves seemed intent on fighting at close quarters which suited Dave. Charnley was clearly winning the fight and was landing often with left hooks. The fight had an unfortunate ending when following a clinch in the 8th round the American emerged with a bad cut over his eye and the referee Tommy Little had no option but to stop the fight. Ringside reporters felt that Gonsalves had perhaps won only a single round up to that point and Charnley would have won convincingly if the fight had continued. Dave told his brother William after the fight that during a clinch in the 1st round Gonsalves had advised Dave that he was going to *carry him*, meaning that he'd let him last the distance! A few rounds later Gonsalves again spoke to Dave in another clinch and warned him that he was going to knock him out. Dave admitted that he was disconcerted at first, but soon realised that Gonsalves wasn't a threat, and began to talk back to the American, whereupon he was warned by Tommy Little.

The importance of this fight was demonstrated in Dave's purse which was £1,750 with a further £149.12s.6d rolling in from the BBC. Board tax was £70, Sparring partners cost him £62, fees for the gym (now back at the Thomas à Beckett) was £15, cornermen cost him £4, £3 again to Bill Chevally for his massages and £461.8s.0d to Arthur Boggis. Dave banked £1,265 and he retained £19 in cash. The promoter gave him £90 worth of tickets.

The comraderie amongst boxers is surprisingly very similar to that enjoyed by golfers. About 40 years after this contest, Dave received a lovely letter out of the blue from Gonsalves. It read 'If Sugar Ray Leonard can come out of retirement and make millions, how about you and I? We would make more than we made at Harringay in 1957. Fond memories of a good night, Sincerely Johnny Gonsalves'.

While Dave was still an apprenticed boilermaker at Vickers he could defer the requirement to enter National Service which at this time was compulsory for all young men in Britain. Seven years had now elapsed, and successful professional boxer or not, Queen and country demanded his services. Just after the Gonsalves fight Dave became Private 23391, Royal Engineers. At his medical examination the British lightweight champion and world top ten ranked fighter was downgraded to level 2, on account of him being flat footed – apparently! His commanding officer, Lieutenant Colonel F G Boswell, an avid boxing fan, decided that Dave should become a Physical Training Instructor and immediately promoted him to Lance-Corporal. He was then posted to Southwood Barracks in Farnborough to begin his two years in the army. As an amazing coincidence Dave found himself joined at Farnborough by childhood friend and distant relative, Jim King, from Craigneuk who was a professional footballer with Hamilton Academicals.

As part of the advice from his accountant Dave reluctantly went out to buy a new Jaguar motor car from Henleys Limited on the 17 June, costing him £1,320. It has to be assumed that this was to offset taxation costs in some way because this would not have been in the quiet, extremely modest Charnley's plans. However this early *Jaguar* experience spoiled Dave, and his future weakness for classy cars would never leave him. Nevertheless Lance-Corporal Charnley must have stuck out like a sore thumb when driving up to the barracks.

On 19 June, World Champion Joe Brown defended his title for the second time with a 15th round knockout of Orlando Zulueta in Denver, Colorado.

South African boxer Willie Toweel came to Britain in the summer of 1957 and apart from a brief spell home remained for the best part of 18 months, fighting top liners on a regular basis. He was a quality, world class performer. Toweel had been the bantamweight, featherweight and currently lightweight champion of his country having failed to win the World bantamweight crown by the narrowest of margins two years earlier drawing with champion Robert Cohen. He had then won the British Empire lightweight title the following year defending it three times. From 32 professional contests he had won 29, drawn twice and lost once.

So on the 9 July at Earls Court Charnley was to challenge for another crown this time the British Empire title. In those days winning the British, Empire and European titles virtually ensured the right to fight for a world title, and this clearly was the route down which Arthur Boggis was taking Dave. Again the Dartford man was fighting a much taller opponent but this time Toweel, unlike Gonsalves, fought from a distance using his long reach to full advantage. As Charnley moved in he would be countered with quick, long punches which landed with jolting accuracy. In the 7th a small cut appeared on Charnley's right eyebrow but it did not cause too many problems at that stage, however, it did galvanise him into greater effort to land his big punches. The 9th was a big round for Dave when his hooks started to land cleanly. Toweel was unsettled and lost his composure momentarily throwing haymakers in desperation. As the fight entered the last third the crowd rose to a frenzy as they cheered their man on, but they were temporarily silenced in the 12th when Toweel landed with a vicious right hand which staggered Dave. He fought back blindly with the referee having to tear them apart at the bell. In the 14th Dave's eye injury opened up again but with the fight nearing its climax there were not too many worries that the fight would be stopped prematurely. In the last round Dave tried his hardest to swing the fight in his favour but still Toweel landed accurately with his right crosses, knocking Dave's head back repeatedly. Welsh referee Ike Powell raised the champions hand at the end and to be fair there were not too many complaints with this result. Daily Mail reporter Harry Carpenter agreed with the decision thinking that Toweel had won by a round. The trade paper,

Boxing News had it wider claiming that there could have been five rounds in it. Dave to this day however still feels he won the fight although brother Joe thought from ringside that not only did Toweel win the fight, but that this was an opponent Dave should not have been paired with so early in his career. However, brother William puts a different slant on things. He says that the following day, Dave told him that after the 12th round, Boggis had said he was well in front and that he should stay out of trouble for the final three rounds. Coasting through these final sessions may have cost him the decision.

For this fight Dave's purse was £2,778 with a further £245 arriving courtesy of the BBC for broadcasting rights. His Board of Control tax was £111 and there was another £76 taken off for other expenses. Arthur Boggis, as manager, took his percentage, £896, with Dave finally banking £2,127.

There was now a level of doubt within the British boxing public as to just how far the young star could go. Was his aggressive hooking style suitable at a higher level? Was he to be an exciting star on the domestic scene only? Promoters Jack Solomons and Harry Levene must have entertained similar thoughts and this was evident when Solomons continued to promote Toweel in this country.

Another difficulty for Dave was his National Service. Although his military bosses were extremely lenient in terms of granting leave, this only kicked in when he was preparing for a fight. Routinely he had to be at camp and while he could keep fit being a PTI, the sharpness he gained from regular sparring and being advised during these sessions by Boggis, Ray Bartlett and others including Danny Holland, was missing. For the quiet, deep thinking Charnley, this was a trying time for him although he never let it show. He remained extremely focussed on the game plan – more titles and more money. It was around this time that Dave sold his interests in his pub to brother William thereby removing another distraction for him.

The new boxing season opened up for Dave on 30 September at the unusual venue of the ice rink in Southampton. His opponent was Joe Woussem who had recently lost the Belgian title in May. On this night Dave was back to his best, totally dominating his game opponent. Woussem appeared to win the 5th round but this was only a temporary blip and he was saved by the bell at the end of the 7th. When the 9th ended referee Jack Morris asked the Belgian if he wanted to continue and the visitor grimly nodded his assent. However, very quickly after the start of the next round the referee stepped in to save the brave fighter from further punishment.

For this routine, marking time fight, Dave earned £475 with sparring partners Barnie Beale and Ernie Fossey costing him £27. The managers cut amounted to £109 with the remainder entering the burgeoning Charnley bank account.

In October Dave knew he was scheduled to fight Ron Hinson the following month. Hinson was four years older than Dave and had engaged in 31 fights, winning 24. During 1957 he had fought Guy Gracia, the Frenchman who had previously beaten Dave twice, and Hinson had won on both occasions. At the end of 1956 he had been ranked as the number seven challenger for the British title and by fight night he had moved up to be the number one contender, making it surprising that, for this fight, Dave's Lonsdale belt was not up for grabs.

The contest took place on 19 November at Earls Court over ten rounds and Dave dominated from start to finish. Hinson, from Dagenham, had some early success but he lacked the physical strength to keep Charnley away. He took a brief trip to the floor in the 8th and, although cut, he managed to see out the fight to the final bell. It was thought at ringside that Hinson never won a round. Perhaps the decision not to bill this as a British title encounter was correct after all.

With Dave now top of the bill on a big London promotion, his purse was back up to the four figure mark at £1,000. Board tax was £40, his chief sparring partners were George Martin and Johnny Lomey who were paid a total of £43 with Boggis's share being £227. Dave banked £680.

On 4 December in Chicago, Joe Brown successfully defended the world lightweight crown against Joey Lopes for the third time.

At the end of the year it was reported that both Jack Solomons and Harry Levene were pulling together to get a world title fight for either Willie Toweel or Dave. Solomons was planning to have Dave fight either Paolo Rossi, Johnny Busso or Kenny Lane early in the new year and a victory could bring about a challenge to Joe Brown on the Eve of the Derby show on 3 June.

In December Dave joined Freddie Mills, Henry Cooper and his brother Jim, at Toby Noble's gym club in Bermondsey to *serve* a slap-up meal to lads from Liverpool who had come down to fight junior boxers from London in a charity event. Once again Dave was reluctantly becoming a sporting celebrity for the press, a situation which made him decidedly uncomfortable.

Sports photographer from that era, Derek Rowe, claims that this shy personality held him back from becoming an even greater household name. Journalists found great difficulty in getting him to open up with statements and comments which they could have exploited and publicised, but Dave has no regrets. Indeed this aspect of his personality has not changed to this day.

Over the course of this year Dave had earned in the region of £6,500 from the ring. Using the purchase price of a new Jaguar motor car at £1,350, as a guideline, it is possible to estimate that £1 in 1957 was worth £19 today. Therefore Dave's fight income is valued at £123,500 in 2011. Not bad for a 22 year old soldier!

Historical Note – 1957
Harold McMillan becomes Prime Minister
Britain tests its first Hydrogen bomb on Christmas Island
Russia launches the first satellite
Patrick Moore presents the first Sky at Night programme on the BBC
The film, The Bridge over the River Kwai, released

CHAPTER 6

Waterman and Ortiz

In 1958 Dave had six fights, three of which would have a profound effect on his immediate future. The first propelled him into the world's top ten, the second made him a massive star in British boxing, and the third brought him crashing down to earth with a massive thump. That was offset by a significant surge in his ring earnings and both manager Arthur Boggis and loyal friend Ray Bartlett still firmly believed they had a future world champion on their hands. At the start of the year though he was still *only* the British lightweight champion with both the Empire and European titles on the radar.

Dave had to bring forward his training schedule when he was alerted to the fact he'd be fighting at the end of January. He knew that Jack Solomons was trying for a top level American opponent but did not know his identity until 15 January when the opposition touched down at London Airport. He was an Apache Indian from Los Angeles and ranked number eight in the world – Don Jordan.

Geronimo, as Jordan was nicknamed, had been in 45 fights winning 35, which included his last six in a row. One of his victims, three months previously, was Orlando Zulueta, who had lost to Joe Brown for the world title in June. Jordan was a top class performer who was intent on moving into contention to fight Brown himself. Being three inches taller than Dave, with a longer reach, he was just the type to give him trouble, similar in style to Willie Toweel.

Dave had a lucky escape in the lead up to the fight. He was driving towards the gym one day in his Jaguar when a lorry coming in the opposite direction misjudged the clearance and ripped the side off the car. Dave was unhurt but the camp kept the matter quiet in case promoter Solomons got to hear about it. So quiet indeed that when the insurance paid up, and a new Jaguar appeared, locals just assumed that this *boxing lark* must be paying handsomely!

Charnley, as usual for successful sportsmen doing National Service, got special leave from the army to prepare at the Thomas à Beckett. In the build up he employed three sparring partners, the lighter and fast moving Derry Treanor, plus slightly bigger lads, George Martin and Leo Maloney. All the national newspapers were speculating that victory in this fight would certainly bring about a world title tilt at Brown and promoter Jack Solomons did nothing to dispel these suggestions.

A few days before the fight Dave and Jordan attended the Boxing Writers dinner at the Criterion Restaurant in Piccadilly Circus as part of the big build up.

At the weigh-in on the day of the fight, held as usual at Solomons gym in Windmill Street, Dave came in at 9st 10lb 4oz, slightly over the lightweight limit, although this was not a requirement on this occasion. In those days there were none of the *in your face* snarling between the fighters which tarnishes the modern game. The boxers simply turned up, stripped off, stood on the scales, got the nod from the Board inspector, said a few words to the press and went off either for a stroll or to a nice restaurant for a steak.

The bout at Harringay was a sell out and the fight crowd were fearful that the tall American might have had too much in his armoury for the 22 year old. The feeling was that Jordan would fight on the outside, be clever defensively and pick off the attacking British champion as he moved in. How wrong they were. Dave did attack as usual but so too did Jordan and this played into the Dartford man's plans.

Jordan tried to cut off the ring and force Charnley into the corners but Dave was becoming more tactically aware keeping on the move and for once was able to counter effectively while going backwards. This was a new, much more skilful Charnley and the fans were seeing a contrast to the no-holds barred, constantly attacking *pocket Marciano*, as he had been christened in some quarters.

In the 2nd round Jordan landed flush with a left and right and the crowd rose when Dave fought back and forced Jordan to the ropes. In the next round Jordan, who constantly edged forward into striking range, was caught by a left hook to the body which clearly troubled him. Charnley recognised his success and this became a pattern for the fight. Charnley was on top but Jordan came back in the 6th when he scored with a heavy body shot followed by a left and right which found Dave's chin. For the remainder of this round Jordan kept on the offensive throwing roundhouse swings as he attempted to take control.

Jordan took the next round as well and the crowd became quieter as their pre-fight fears looked like materialising. The 8th was much more even and could have gone either way but right at the bell Dave went stumbling down onto his back. Many at ringside thought Dave had been knocked down, however, the confusion arose because it appeared that referee Eugene Henderson had been over zealous when prising the boxers out of a clinch, as Jordan fell at the same time. There was no count administered and Charnley seemed unfazed.

Dave came on in the last two rounds and seemed to win them although they were close. As the fight neared the final bell the Harringay crowd were on their feet cheering on their favourite and at the end, referee Henderson strode over and raised Charnley's arm.

This was a momentous victory, certainly his best performance to date, and according to Dave himself maybe the best performance of his career. Jordan would go on to win the world welterweight title thus demonstrating the significance of Dave's victory. He had shown that he could adapt his tactics and was maturing as a fighter. Everyone in British boxing now believed that he was the country's best chance of securing a world championship.

Dave's purse for this fight was £1,600 and with no television coverage, there were nothing extra from broadcasting rights on this occasion. Board tax was £64, and to emphasize the importance of his preparations for this fight sparring partners cost him £140 (£3,000 at today's valuation!). Manager Boggis took £376, and Dave finally banked £960.

On the same night Peter Waterman, the brother of actor Denis, beat Italian Emilio Marconi to win the European welterweight title, a result which would have some bearing for Dave's future plans.

No one can now remember who first suggested a bout between the reigning British and European welterweight champion, Peter Waterman, and Dave Charnley the British champion at the weight below. It was probably promoter Jack Solomons and for this idea 'Jolly Jack' has to take first prize! The fans and the media immediately accepted the prospect with great relish. It became a complete sell-out weeks in advance and the only loser at the end of the day, rather sadly, was Peter Waterman. Surprisingly, even in those days when boxers fought more regularly, Dave, or should it be Boggis, accepted another fight in the interim.

On 11 March, Dave was destined to face Frenchman Tony Garcia, not to be confused with previous foe, Guy Gracia, at Streatham Ice Rink. For this fight Dave hired as sparring partners Peter Cobblah and Jack Armstrong, two strong Ghanians, and Derry Treanor. Cobblah in fact was still fighting in Las Vegas as a light middleweight in 1973!

With the Waterman fight looming the only issue to be resolved was the duration of the contest. Waterman was seeking to fight over the twelve rounds with Dave wanting the shorter ten. In what was obviously a publicity stunt a journalist decided the distance by tossing a coin in the ring prior to the Garcia fight. The outcome of this unusual process was a twelve round contest and Peter Waterman was at ringside to add to the build up.

Dave obviously was not distracted by the forthcoming Waterman fight because the Garcia contest was one-way traffic from start to finish. The Frenchman tried to run and counter but his tactics failed miserably. His punches were short and he was punished by a fighter in top form. Charnley displayed the full repertoire, jabs, hooks and even uppercuts. Poor Peter Waterman must have begun to doubt he was doing the right thing. By the middle of the 4th round only bravery was keeping Garcia going and when he rose from a slip, Charnley battered him across the ring. The 5th started the way the 4th had finished with Dave landing with every punch in his arsenal before, at long last, referee Jack Hart stepped in and brought this slaughter to an end.

For this routine fight Dave was paid £800, with sparring partners costing £80, his Board tax was £32 and the manager's cut being £162. For some reason, in this contest, Dave had to buy his own gloves which cost £11 guineas. He banked £487.

It was reported, after this fight, that Dave's commanding officer at the Royal Engineers promoted him to the rank of Lance-Corporal, but this may have been misinterpreted by the media who obviously didn't realise that he already held this rank by virtue of his position as PTI. A further distraction Dave had to endure before the fight even started was when the usual musical fanfare failed to work properly. For some reason his 18 year old brother Joe and a friend from Dartford had found themselves inside a room high up in the stands which usually played the music during ice hockey matches. When the fanfare music was put on and the searchlights picked out Dave, *the friend* sat down on the turntable and broke the mechanism!

Dave admits today that he never held any animosity towards an opponent, youth, amateur of professional – except one, Peter Waterman, and he finds it difficult to explain why. Waterman always appeared aloof within boxing circles. He expected to be treated better than other boxers and thought himself more intelligent. People got the impression that Waterman considered himself superior in some way. At the Thomas à Beckett, which they both shared as a gym, he carried on as if he owned the place, and on fight nights he always wanted to be treated as the *star attraction.* This type of attitude may be more prevalent today but in the 1950s it was virtually unheard of. Having said all that, Dave maintains that at the time the newspapers blew the rivalry out of all proportion. He didn't hate Waterman he just felt he was arrogant. Dave can clearly recall being in Waterman's company when the fight was first suggested. Waterman openly declared that the idea of him fighting the smaller man, whom he also considered less than capable, was a farce and not worth considering further. Dave, as usual, didn't say a word, but admits now that internally he thought – 'Come on then!'.

The national newspaper build up started at least a week before the fight. Boxing News correspondent Gilbert Odd discovered that while Waterman was still training daily at the Beckett, under the watchful eye of Snowy Buckingham, he was also visiting another unknown London gym in the evenings, sparring with up and coming Walworth prospect, Eddie Hughes. The sessions between Hughes, a southpaw like Charnley, and Waterman were overseen by Solly Cantor the former Canadian lightweight.

The main talking point in the press was the difference in weights. The match was made at 10st 9lb, two pounds over the welterweight limit to ensure that Waterman's British title would not be on the line. It had also been announced that no official weights would be released, only that both fighters weighed in within the stipulated limit. It was being speculated that come fight time Waterman would outweigh Charnley by nearly a stone. Some newspapermen also felt that since Waterman's defeat to the great Kid Gavilan his punch resistance had gone, and they exhorted him to come into the fight in top physical condition.

On the day of the fight eminent reporter Reg Gutteridge was leaning towards a Charnley victory but didn't actually come out and say it. Desmond Hackett was more forthcoming and stated that he felt 'Charnley can give away half a stone and still beat Waterman'. Harry Carpenter writing for the Daily Mail supported Hackett and wrote 'I plump for Charnley on points. With luck we may see what promises on paper to be one of the classic battles of 1958'. LN Bailey had interviewed both managers about the weight issue. Waterman's manager Sam Burns thought his man would come into the ring at 10st 11lb while Arthur Boggis believed Dave would weigh 9st 13lb. Bailey came down on the side of a Waterman victory. George Whiting believed that the fight would go into the later rounds and just edged with the bookmakers who made Charnley a 6-4 favourite. Peter Wilson writing for the Daily Mirror was much more emphatic when he wrote 'So I am picking Charnley to win'.

At lunchtime on the 15 April, both fighters made their way to Solomons gym for the weigh-in. Dave turned up wearing a heavy overcoat and pretended to step on the scales with it still on. However he jumped on, and quickly off, as soon as the bar stopped short of the limit so no one became aware of his true weight for this fight. After Waterman also made the weight Dave and his entourage quickly left the scene and made their way to Boggis's usual city centre restaurant for a steak meal. When the meal was over Dave and Boggis went along with what was now their usual pre-fight routine – a quick sleep in Boggis's Kensington apartment followed by a long taxi ride to the north London venue.

When they arrived at Harringay some two hours before the scheduled 9.30 start time they were acutely aware of the tension that was building from the 11,000 in attendance. Some of Dave's many busloads of supporters waited outside to wish him well when he arrived and shortly after settling into his dressing room, brothers Joe and William came in and offered encouragement. Displaying his natural modesty Dave admits that he had no doubts about the outcome and as was usually the case he got up on the massage bench and fell asleep. He only came to when awoken to begin his warm up.

This proved to be the fight which defined Dave Charnley as the most exciting boxer in Britain for at least the next four years and the main box office attraction for a bit longer. The fight which was shown on BBC's Sportsview programme the following night allowed him to become a household name and one of the best known faces in the country. The *fall-guy* in all this was the unfortunate Peter Waterman, who although he still retained his British and European titles, and still aged only 23 years, never boxed again, such was the thrashing he took.

By the end of the 1st round Waterman was bleeding for a nose injury and in the 2nd he was cut over the right eye and took a sustained beating. The slaughter continued in the 3rd with referee Ike Williams warning Waterman for holding. The 4th was a better round for Waterman, but this was only the appearance of a gap in the clouds before the thunderstorm broke. In the next round Charnley began picking his punches which saw Waterman's head being jolted repeatedly. Towards the end of the round Dave struck. He caught Waterman with a right lead and followed this with a devastating left uppercut. Waterman fell into the ropes with his arms dropping to his side. With this Charnley launched a merciless barrage of hooks to an open target and the massacre continued before the referee belatedly stepped in and pulled Dave off his stricken opponent. Waterman staggered drunkenly to his own corner where the ropes stopped him from falling down. Looking back Dave feels the referee should have intervened far sooner. This was a momentous victory for Charnley and his supporters cheered until they were hoarse.

Once the excitement had died down and Dave was showered and got his breath back, he was able to have a few moments of quiet reflection giving thought to his beaten opponent. All the bad feelings towards Waterman had gone and Dave didn't like the idea of going home without letting him know this. He told Arthur Boggis that he wanted to go to the other dressing room and once they had fought their way past the reporters Dave was able to shake Waterman's hand and offer his condolences.

It was then straight home to Thanet Road Bexley where a warm bath was waiting for him. There were never any *after fight* parties for Dave, he just wasn't in the mood. He could never understand how some fighters enjoyed this because he was always in so much muscular pain from his exertions.

For this fight Dave earned £2,500 purse money, £95 for the

radio rights and £124 from BBC. £70 went on sparring partners, £100 to the Board and £624 to Arthur Boggis. Dave eventually banked £1,874.

Immediately after the fight Waterman's manager Sam Burns, his advisor Jarvis Astaire, and corner man Mickey Duff all suggested that he should retire. Before the fight he had pencilled in a defence of his European title against Emilio Marconi which would have secured a £4,000 pay day but no one, not even the man himself thought he should go on. It was a sad way to end, what was, a very successful career.

Sitting at ringside was Angelo Dundee who would later become famous as the trainer of Muhammed Ali and Sugar Ray Leonard, amongst others. Dundee said that Charnley was definitely world class and good enough to fight any lightweight in the world including champion, Joe Brown, a view shared by Jack Solomons. Manager Boggis now had several options to consider. Prior to the fight Dave had been nominated to fight Duilio Loi for the European lightweight title, and Boggis was intent on travelling to Milan on 27 April to see him fight in a non-title contest. At the same time, in the immediate aftermath of the Waterman fight, Boggis was also suggesting that Charnley should take Waterman's place and fight Marconi for the welterweight championship. Either way Dave's career was scaling new heights.

On 7 May Joe Brown successfully defended his world title in Houston, Texas by beating Ralph Dupas on a technical knockout in the eighth round.

When someone becomes a bit of a celebrity it is interesting to observe how the media can create an image for that person based on their own interpretations. Some journalists had started to refer to Dave as *sullen* and *moody* giving the impression he was perhaps a temperamental and aggressive young man. The truth is that Dave was agonisingly shy and didn't like talking about himself. Indeed he is the same to this day. Reg Gutteridge got to know him as well as anybody in the media and it is clear from his articles that he had identified this characteristic. On some of his longer articles it was Dave's wife Ruth who provided the most information.

On the fighting front it was still being reported that Dave was due to fight Duilio Loi by the 27 June for the European crown. Around this time photographer Derek Rowe remembers a situation which emphasizes the influence Ray Bartlett still had over Dave even though he had no official involvement. A crowd of fight people were sitting downstairs in the Thomas à Beckett when Dave was summoned upstairs to speak to Arthur Boggis on the phone. When he came back down Ray Bartlett asked what Boggis was wanting. Dave replied that he had arranged a fight with Loi. On hearing this Bartlett told Dave that he should not be fighting him and to tell Boggis that he was refusing. Dave went back upstairs and phoned his manager. A short time later he returned telling the assembled company that contracts had been signed and that if the fight didn't go ahead they'd be sued. Funnily enough Dave never did fight Loi!

As it became clear that a fight with Loi was disappearing into the mist both Boggis and Jack Solomons were keen to keep their prize asset in the public eye. Solomons always ran an Eve of the Derby show each June and he quickly arranged a top of the bill bout for the British and Empire heavyweight title between Joe

Erskine and Brian London. Supporting this was a contest between Dave and Joe Lopes.

This was an inspired piece of matchmaking. Lopes had boxed a non-title draw with champion Joe Brown twelve months previously a result which earned him a bash at the ultimate prize itself. That fight took place in December when Lopes was stopped in the 11th round. The fighter who was born in Portugal but now resident in California was still ranked number five in the world although he had also recently lost to rising star, Carlos Ortiz. Lopes arrived at London Airport on24 May and remarked to waiting reporters that this was his second visit to Britain having served part of his time as a Sergeant in the US Air Force at Uxbridge.

The fight on 3 June was the first time Dave had fought at the White City and it turned out to be a successful visit. The White City was only half full due to a bus strike in London and there had been arguments beforehand between Jack Solomons and Arthur Boggis over the purse. Eventually Boggis backed down due to the reduced gate money.

Lopes turned out to be a tough opponent but he was not as sharp as his Californian friends Jordan and Gonsalves had been. He tried to counter punch but his blows lacked the sharpness necessary. Dave really took over the fight in the 4th round when a left hook sent Lopes to the canvas for a count of four. The visitor jumped up too quickly and almost paid the penalty with Charnley swarming all over him. He returned to his corner with a badly cut eyebrow. Dave was winning the fight comfortably and appeared to be boxing within himself. This casualness cost him dearly with almost the last punch of the fight when a Lopes punch opened a cut above his right eye. Referee Jack Hart quickly strode over at the bell to award Charnley the fight with Lopes shaking his head in disbelief. Ringside reporters didn't give the Californian a round on their scorecards.

Dave's purse for this fight was £2,500. Sparring partners cost him £82, Danny Vary had now appeared on the scene as a trainer, and his fee was £50 and Boggis's share was £590. Dave banked £1,775.

As had become the norm after a fight, Dave returned to the lonely existence of his life at the barracks in Farnborough. There Dave clearly enjoyed a privileged position in comparison to others but with his determination to run at 5.30 each morning and the disruption this caused, Colonel Boswell decided that Dave should sleep in an annex to the gymnasium. This was a large room with a coal fire and became home after the day's business. When the recruits had gone no one else shared this accommodation and Dave was left on his own. He was allowed to return to Bexley each weekend however, and this became important to him because he missed the company.

There were also changes in Dave's business plans. Brother William and his wife Eileen decided to use some of the money they had garnered from managing the pub to buy a confectionary shop in Gravesend. Due to this Dave gave up his rental agreement with the brewers and his days as a publican were over.

On 23 July in Houston, Texas once again, Joe Brown successfully defended his world title for the fifth time against Kenny Lane with a points decision over 15 rounds.

With the Loi fight inextricably delayed until September

Boggis moved quickly to secure an interim contest in Liverpool against Scottish welterweight Jimmy Croll. However disaster struck when Dave contracted a severe gastric influenza, which not only put paid to the Croll match, but forced another delay to the European title bid in Milan. This was now re-scheduled for 29 November.

Dave was committed to fighting for the Liverpool Stadium promoter Johnny Best and the fight with Croll went ahead on 18 September. Dave, Boggis and Dave Crowley, who was training him for this fight, all arrived in Liverpool the day before. Boggis was disappointed that no one was at Liverpool Station to meet them and immediately set about finding Best. The reason for this was clear. Boggis had agreed a purse with Best which was based on 35% of the gate and with little apparent interest being shown in the fight he saw a good pay day going to waste. The weigh-in unusually for a Liverpool Stadium fight was held in the hotel at which both boxers were staying. Dave weighed a career heaviest 9st 13lb. After the weigh-in Dave met up with older brother William and both spent the afternoon at a local cinema.

On their arrival at the Stadium Boggis's worst fears were realised with only around 1,000 people in attendance. Dave, having been out the ring for over three months, looked sluggish but was always in control over the Dundee fighter who out-weighed him by 6lb. In the 3rd round Charnley recoiled from a clash of heads leaving Croll with a bad cut over his left eye. In the next round a slashing one-two opened an horrendous gash on Croll's left cheek and when he returned to his corner manager Tommy Gilmour Snr summoned over the referee and pulled his fighter out. Afterwards Croll graciously commented that Charnley was the greatest opponent he had ever faced and also the hardest punching.

Dave received a staggeringly small purse of £370 for this fight with the Board tax being £30, sparring partners costing him £15, and Dave Crowley received £40. Boggis only took £58 but Dave still had to pay the hotel bill! For his journey north Dave banked £175.

Harringay Arena in north London had been a famous old fight venue since 1936 when Syd Hulls promoted there, but sadly for boxing fans, it was about to be turned into a warehouse. Jack Solomons had used the place for all his big promotions since 1946 and now he would need to find somewhere else. The final show at the venue was scheduled for 28 October and Solomons planned to make it a gala occasion. Many of the top quality boxers who had fought there, both from Britain and elsewhere, were invited to attend – and most did. Included amongst these were former world heavyweight champion Max Baer and former triple weight champion, Henry Armstrong.

But, top of the bill, with pride of place was the fight between Dave Charnley and New Yorker Carlos Ortiz. When the fight was announced Dave was ranked number three in the world with Ortiz one place behind. Ortiz, aged 22 years, was born in Puerto Rico, but took up boxing when the family moved to Manhattan in 1944. Ortiz had boxed in Britain previously in 1953 when he fought Georgie Guy from East Ham in a New York versus London amateur competition. In 30 contests to date Ortiz had only lost once to Johnny Busso, a result later avenged.

In the build up to the fight Dave again used the services of Dave Crowley and sparred many rounds with George Martin, Ernie Fossey and Johnny Fish. The press clearly favoured a Charnley victory but they were basing this assessment purely on his previous wins over Lopes, Jordan and Gonsalves. They were already speculating on the proposed European title tilt at Duilio Loi, which was still scheduled for the end of November, and a world title challenge to Joe Brown early in the new year.

Unknown to anyone outside the camp Dave had injured his left hand ten days before the fight and all sparring had to be stopped. It is possible that this happened when in the ring with Ernie Fossey, because Ernie only got paid for two rounds of sparring instead of the usual three. At any rate Dave was taken to a doctor who said there were no broken bones as far as he could tell.

On the night of the fight Harringay, as expected, was full to its 11,000 capacity with the BBC cameras also present. While Ortiz was warming up in his dressing room the Charnley camp were in a state of near panic. Not only was Dave carrying an injury to his left hand but his right was now causing problems. A doctor administered nine pain killing injections to Dave's injured hands. Such was the scale of the problem that Boggis approached Jack Solomons asking for Dave to be taken off the bill. The promoter just couldn't agree to this given the circumstances of the night. Dave made no excuse at the time because that was simply not in his nature, but he remembers the unusual sensation of his hands inside the gloves and them feeling like a lumps of wood.

Dave's brother William recalls the circumstances vividly. He had been used to accumulating bets from former patrons of his pub and backing Dave at a local bookmakers. On this night he had gathered up around £1,000 (£20,000 at today's prices) and because his local man wouldn't accept the bet, he was intent on betting at the ringside. When he arrived at Harringay he met his brother Joe who had just came from Dave's dressing room. Joe asked if he had put the bet on yet, and William was told about the problem with the hands. William wouldn't elaborate about whether he did take the gamble!!

The fight was a disaster for all concerned. Dave was outboxed from beginning to end and most reporters had him winning only the 4th round. His nose bled for most of the fight and from the 7th round onward he had also to contend with a one inch cut along his eyebrow. Ortiz simply had Charnley's number. He scored consistently with long right hands which always seemed to land on target and when inside he could hook with the best of them. Dave simply didn't have the answers and looked a disconsolate fighter at the bell. The fight film gives the impression that Ortiz was so much bigger than Dave, and the Dartford man was unable to force the New Yorker backwards in order to get leverage into his punches.

Boggis tried to make excuses after the fight claiming that the injured hand had been the problem, and some journalists joined in suggesting that his stomach illness during the summer, coupled with the long layoff, effected his timing. Dave now reluctantly admits that his injured hands threw him completely out of his stride and was a distraction he simply couldn't overcome. Nevertheless Ortiz was a magnificent fighter and would perform at the top of his game for many years to come.

No matter how it was viewed this was a major setback to Dave's world title aspirations.

He was compensated somewhat with a £3,000 purse and the £199 he received from the BBC. Outgoings included £120 Board tax, £93 for sparring partners, £50 to his trainer Dave Crowley, and £734 to Arthur Boggis. £2,202 went into the Charnley bank account.

With the result and injuries to his hand and eyebrow there was no way Dave could fight Loi on 29 November, and indeed his fighting for the year was over. Towards the end of November he went private and paid £46 for an operation to his hand at the London Clinic.

Although still doing National Service, Dave's earnings before expenses from his boxing career during the year amounted to £11,200, an equivalent today of around £212,000. Now 23 years of age and with only six months to go before his National Service was complete, the damaged hand and the loss to Ortiz must have raised serious doubts about his boxing future.

Historical Note – 1958
Gatwick Airport opens
Munich Air disaster sees Manchester United players and officials killed
'My Fair Lady' starring Rex Harrison and Julie Andrews opens in Drury Lane
Bolton Wanderers win the FA cup
Ultrasound scanning first introduced

CHAPTER 7

British Empire Champion

Dave Charnley's aim in life was to win the world title and earn as much from the old fight game as he could in the process. It could be argued that his career up to 1959 including all those long forgotten, schools, youth and amateur bouts were preparing him for that day. His chance would come at last towards the end of the year but he had a few hurdles to jump beforehand with some notable successes.

In the previous two years January had been a crucial month for Dave with big wins over Willie Lloyd and then Don Jordan. With the loss to Ortiz still on his mind he would have wished for an early chance to redeem himself but he had to cool his heels until 10 March. Although the media were still talking up a challenge to Loi for the European title this fight was never really on manager Boggis's agenda. Promoter Harry Levene had booked Wembley for this early spring date with his heavyweight hope Brian London destined to top the bill. However panic set in when London injured his back and had to withdraw. Levene quickly phoned Johannesburg seeking the services of former opponent Guy Gracia who was in South Africa fighting Willie Toweel. Gracia's manager Pierre Louis immediately accepted the offer. It was a match Boggis, and Dave, were keen to accept.

On 11 February Joe Brown retained his world title for the

6th time with a points decision over Johnny Busso in Houston, Texas.

It had been three years since Garcia had beaten Charnley and there was a personal need for this result to be avenged. Garcia was a quality fighter and no stranger to British shores. He had arrived twelve times previously and left as the victor on nine occasions. By fight time Gracia was 36 years of age, but looking at him and recording his performances in recent fights nobody could have believed it.

On the 10 March therefore, full-house signs were again the order of the day at Wembley as the Charnley fan club turned up in their thousands in great expectation. The fight itself was pretty tame with the Frenchman moving away happily behind a high guard and throwing very little leather. On the other hand, although Dave started slowly, he was still finding the occasional gap in Gracia's defence to score regularly. From the 5th onward Charnley began to loosen up and by the start of the 10th was well on top. Gracia came out smiling as if to imply that the Dartford Destroyer had not destroyed him! When the final bell rang Gracia came over to Charnley and appeared to congratulate him, however a bigger fight was about to commence because Bradford referee Fred Blakeborough gave the decision to Gracia. Journalist Desmond Hackett at ringside provided an unbeatable account of what happened. 'Charnley's manager Arthur Boggis leaped into the ring, snatched the scorecard from the referee and handed it to Boxing Board secretary Teddy Waltham. There was more desperate fighting around the ringside than took place inside it, as fans stamped, jeered and hissed their protests at the verdict. Burly stewards hustled in to bustle the referee through the threatening crowd that moved menacingly up. It was an ugly scene, a moment that poised on the dangerous, delicate balance of a riot. Back in his dressing room Charnley savagely tore off his crimson gloves, hurled them against the whitewashed wall and snarled 'I have finished with that lot for good. Unless I get satisfaction from the Boxing Board I will never fight again. They can keep my title, I am not standing for this.'

The jeers at ringside continued well after the start of the next bout and gangs of supporters raged through the corridors at Wembley apparently looking for the referee. It appeared to be a horrendous decision. The following morning all the national boxing writers, except one, had Charnley winning clearly, with most giving Gracia only one round. There was considerable discussion as to what could be done, because clearly the Boxing Board could not reverse the referee's decision. By this time however, Dave had rescinded his previous statement that he would never fight again.

The following day, amidst unprecedented scenes, Don Service, Secretary of the Dave Charnley supporters club, along with 20 friends and members of Dave's family called at the offices of the Boxing Board of Control and handed in a petition signed by hundreds of fans demanding the decision be annulled. Board Secretary, Teddy Waltham came out to meet them and advised that the proper way of doing things was for Dave's manager to put any complaints in writing. Mr Service told the waiting press that over 2,000 fans went regularly to Charnley fights, and although beaten previously by Carlos Ortiz and Willie Toweel, they had never felt so aggrieved. Arthur Boggis on learning of Teddy Waltham's comment duly called at the Board offices with his lawyer and Dave, to hand deliver his letter of apology for entering the ring and demanding an enquiry. Boggis also told the waiting press that he was considering taking legal action.

So what really happened? National newspapers in those days had writers who specifically concentrated on boxing and attended almost every major contest. It can be argued that boxing was perhaps the second most popular sport in the country and to support this assertion, trade paper, the Boxing News sold 250,000 copies every week. These reporters it has to be argued, knew their stuff. Peter Wilson was absolutely outraged at the decision, while Reg Gutteridge thought Charnley won, but he had seen much worse verdicts. Steve Fagan and Donald Saunders were as outraged as Peter Wilson but Gerard Walters believed Gracia had just edged it. The Boxing News correspondent was so incensed by the decision he thought about joining in with the protests! It doesn't matter now of course because the record books show another Charnley loss.

When the dust had settled Dave earned £2,400 plus £71 this time from ITN who filmed the fight. Board tax was £96, with training expenses being £307. The manager's cut was £517. Dave banked £1,500.

When all the furore had died down, and Arthur Boggis had paid his £250 Board fine for pulling Fred Blakeborough's scorecard out of his hand, Dave and his manager had a problem. They knew that when the telegrams reached Joe Brown's promoter and manager after the Gracia fight they would in all probability have dismissed Charnley as a challenger for the world title. However lady luck eventually began to turn her compassionate face on the Dartford man. As a matter of interest Fred Blakeborough never refereed another fight.

Harry Levene had booked the Empire Pool, Wembley for a contest between recent Charnley conquerors, Carlos Ortiz and Willie Toweel, on 12 May. This was destined to be an unofficial eliminator for Joe Brown's crown. Ortiz held the number one contender's position while Toweel was ranked five places below. But Ortiz suffered a bad eye injury when fighting Lennie Matthews and had to call off leaving the promoter with very few options. It now seems natural that he should have chosen Dave to fight Toweel for the British Empire title and here was an opportunity for Charnley to kill two birds with the one stone. A chance to win another title and at the same time grab the South African's world ranking.

Dave was certainly not slacking in the build up to this contest because a week before the fight he broke the ribs of sparring partner Eddie West from Bethnal Green. West had to be taken to Paddington Hospital and was withdrawn from his forthcoming fight with Robbie Wilson at Shoreditch. Dave would later admit that following his stomach illness, his damaged right hand and injured elbow made him doubt whether he would ever be fully fit again, so he worked flat out on his sparring partners to convince himself he was back to his best. Reporters visiting the Thomas à Beckett noticed that uncharacteristically Dave was short with other members of his camp. Meanwhile Toweel was using southpaw Eddie Hughes from the Fitzroy Lodge gym in preparation.

Not surprising given Dave's recent form there were few in the press who thought he would win. Toweel had recently undergone a sinus operation and had beaten Gracia in January. He arrived back in Britain several weeks before the fight and felt at home given the amount of time he had spent in London over the preceeding twelve months. Charnley meanwhile appeared to be on a downslide and another defeat would surely end all hopes of a world title opportunity.

The first sign of problems for Toweel occurred at the 1pm weigh-in held at Joe Bloom's gym. Toweel was ten ounces overweight. He had his second Turkish bath of the day and returned quarter of an hour later still four ounces over the limit. He finally shed this by 1.30pm but this was a worrying sign.

Once again Dave's fans helped fill the Empire Pool for this make or break battle and they were not to be disappointed. He turned in a performance of a lifetime to wrench the Empire title from a brave champion. From the very first bell Charnley stalked his skilful opponent and whenever he found himself within range he let the punches fly. He was winning the fight comfortably and Toweel had nothing in his arsenal to hold him off. In the 8th round however the fans saw an unexpected comeback with the South African starting to find his form, with long left jabs and right uppercuts finding their mark. His joy was short lived because Charnley came out determined to keep control in the 9th and near the end of the round, Toweel emerged from a clinch with a very bad cut over his right eye. Toweel's cornerman Danny Holland patched him up as best as he could but the very first punch of the 10th, a left hook, re-opened the injury, and sensing the *kill* Dave stormed after the retreating champion. At the two minute mark Charnley caught Toweel with a shuddering left hook which shook him to his bootlaces. A short right and another left dropped him to a knee. Referee Andrew Smyth counted to ten before Toweel regained his feet and a new Empire champion was crowned. Charnley had clearly learned from his mistakes in the first fight and repeatedly caught Toweel with short right hooks when he led off with his left.

Dave earned a purse of £3,000 with another £207 arriving from the television coverage. The Board tax came to £120, his training expenses were £250, with the manager's cut was £684. Dave banked £2,000.

On 3 June Joe Brown successfully defended his world title for the seventh time with a 9th round stoppage of Paolo Rosi in Washington DC.

It had always been a hope of Dave's to fight up in Scotland so that his relatives and friends in Craigneuk could get to see him on home soil. He was delighted that Glasgow promoter Sammy Docherty could put on a show and pleased also that Arthur Boggis accepted the terms offered. The fight was arranged for 17 June outdoors at Firhill Park in Glasgow, home of Partick Thistle football club.

Dave reached the end of his National Service the previous week and had intended to drive through France to Italy for a well deserved break. Accordingly with all these arrangements to be made, Dave could only arrive with wife Ruth the day before the fight, flying into Renfrew Airport and being whisked straight off to his hotel. He did not forget his friends however and they all got complementary ringside tickets. His opponent was former British featherweight champion from Londonderry, Billy 'Spider' Kelly.

Although only 28 years old Kelly's career was on the wane, but he was not someone to be taken lightly. The fight was made at 9st 11lb and both made the limit easily. A very healthy 7,000 spectators were in attendance and all the Scottish based newspapers had lengthy articles in the days leading up to the contest, obviously concentrating on Dave's Scottish background. Unfortunately Dave's brother William remembers that mention had been made during the build up of the fact that their grandmother Bella Fraser was the Worthy Mistress of the ladies section of the Orange Order. With Spider Kelly being an Irish Catholic, the West of Scotland disease, sectarianism, reared its head and as Dave walked to the ringside William heard abuse of this nature being directed towards his brother. Unfortunately this greatly anticipated fight turned out to be a bit of a letdown, particularly the unsatisfactory nature of the ending.

Charnley boxed well within himself but opened up with combinations on occasion clearly hurting Kelly. Spider was known to bob and weave but for most of this contest he was ducking well below the waistline due to an inability to avoid Charnley's attacks. Kelly was warned repeatedly about this by referee Frank Wilson. Near the end of the 4th round Kelly had to take a brief count from a right hand but didn't seem to be in any danger of being stopped. In the 6th, with Kelly continuously ducking low, the referee stepped in and disqualified the Irishman. The crowd erupted and when the referee left the ring, a fan tried to punch him before being bundled away by the police. It had not been a vintage Charnley performance but he had fulfilled a long held ambition by fighting in front of his people in Scotland.

Dave's purse was £1,750, with outgoings including Board tax of £70, training and travelling expenses of £283 and £349 going to his manager. Dave banked a nice round figure of £1,000.

Over the summer Arthur Boggis was pushing for a world title tilt at Joe Brown but neither of the big London promoters, Solomons and Levene, could entice the champion to cross the Atlantic. Boggis also thought that the time was right for his charge, but knew that taking on any other major contenders in the meantime could jeopardise this opportunity. Tentative agreement was reached with Brown's manager Lou Viscusi for a fight towards the end of the year, in the States, but Dave would need some fight action before then.

Therefore Boggis readily accepted Belfast man Jimmy Brown as the opponent at Streatham Ice Rink on 1 September. It has to be said that Brown posed no threat to Charnley, being a light puncher, but he could provide a good workout. That was how it turned out but the press were totally unimpressed afterwards.

The contest, promoted by Stan Baker, lasted almost eight one-sided rounds before referee Tommy Little stopped the beating. In the 1st round Dave scored at will and near the end of that session a strong left uppercut nearly put Brown down. Some reporters noted that the uppercut was not thrown again until the last round, using this fact to justify their assertions that Charnley *carried* his opponent. The following day in the national press most of the established boxing writers were writing off Dave's chances for the world title, suggesting that if he didn't have the punch to stop Jimmy Brown, he would have no chance of stopping namesake Joe! The about turn from their positions following Dave's fights with Guy Gracia and Willie

Toweel was surprising, and there seems no logical explanation unless they believed they were being short-changed in some way.

There was an unusual aside to this bout. While the boxers were waiting for the fight to get underway, the announcer invited several ex-fighters up into the ring to receive the applause of the crowd. One of them was Peter Waterman. When he went over towards Dave for the customary handshake, he put his hand across his chest in a manner which poked fun at Dave's apparent lack of height. Waterman may have thought he was simply making a joke, but Dave was livid inside and remarked upon this after the fight.

For this contest Dave earned £1,200 and £37 came from television. The board tax was £48, his training expenses were £215, and his managers slice was £243. He banked £700.

The world lightweight rankings were announced around this time. The champion was Joe Brown with contenders, in order, being Carlos Ortiz, Kenny Lane, Dave Charnley, Paolo Rosi, Johnny Busso, Lennie Matthews, Johnny Gonsalves, Rafael Torres, Paul Armstead and Mauro Vasquez.

On 16 October Dave signed a contract to fight Joe Brown for the world title in Houston, Texas on 2 December. The contract entitled Dave to 20% of the live gate plus additional revenue from television and film rights. Jack Solomons who was co-promoting the fight estimated that Dave would net around £7,500 (roughly £142,500 at today's prices). At last he had fulfilled his lifetime's ambition.

On 24 October, Dave and brother Joe set off for the Corn Exchange in King's Lynn for a charity exhibition bout between Dave and Canning Town's Jimmy Daly. In order to drum up support the press were suggesting that Daly may not quite appreciate the status of the *fight* given that Dave had apparently broken his jaw while sparring in the Thomas à Beckett during July. Dave had to rush home after this event because wife Ruth was to be a maid of honour at Chelsea footballer Peter Brabook's wedding at which Jimmy Greaves was the best man.

Preparations were now being made to travel to America for the opportunity of a lifetime.

CHAPTER 8

First World Title Challenge

In 1959 there were only eight weight divisions in professional boxing. The lightest category was flyweight which included boxers up to 8st. At the other end of the scale were the heavyweights who weighed over 12st 7lb.

A boxer could only win the world title by beating the man considered to be the champion. There had been a few occasions up to that point when the identity of who was the actual champion might be in dispute, but these were rare and usually involved Europe and America having conflicting views. These disagreements were sorted by a fight between the two to settle matters.

In the lightweight 9st 9lb division the universally accepted champion at this time was Joe Brown. You will have noticed regular mentions of his title defences up till now. He could trace the lineage of the lightweight title back to 6 October 1872 when Arthur Chambers beat Billy Edwards on a thirty fifth round disqualification at Squirrel Island in the United States.

Brown was officially recorded as being 33 years of age but considered by many to be much older. That's why he had earned the nickname 'Old Bones'. He was born and brought up in Baton Rouge, Louisiana one of a family of three children and attended Mc Kinley High school where he excelled in baseball and basketball. He followed his father into carpentry and didn't leave home until he joined the US Navy during the Second World War. The ship he was on took part in seven Pacific landings. Brown took up boxing during this period and won the Navy lightweight championship winning all sixteen contests.

He was married soon after leaving the navy in 1948 and had four children. After his duty in the services, Brown worked in a pharmacy and then a car bumper repair garage in Chicago. When his professional boxing career began the family were living in New Orleans but had since re-located to Houston, Texas. In the early years of the decade Lou Viscusi became his manager. This was the same man who guided the career of the brilliant featherweight champion Willie Pep. Up to this point Brown had taken part in an incredible 103 bouts, winning 75, 35 of which were inside the distance victories. He had drawn 10 and there were 2 no-contests. He had been stopped on only 3 occasions. Old Bones had lost once in his last 24 fights, a points defeat to Johnny Busso, in a ten round non-title contest.

Brown's fight with Dave would be his eighth defence of the title he won from Wallace 'Bud' Smith in August 1956. Of his previous seven victims only two had lasted the distance.

Once details of the fight had been arranged Dave set about his preparations in earnest. On almost a daily basis his training at the Thomas à Beckett included nine rounds of sparring. Ray Bartlett had organised these sessions so that each aspect of Dave's fight plan could be worked on. For speed work he brought in bantamweight George Dormer, for strength welterweight Butch Davis, and for skill featherweight Terry Rees. Ray then arranged for Rees to box rounds one, four and seven. Davis boxed rounds two, five and eight. Poor George

Dormer boxed the others. Brave George was put on his back every single day he sparred, but he never stopped coming. Each boxer was paid £9 for his day's work, George didn't get any extra! Terry Rees vividly remembers being caught on the chin by a left uppercut which drove his top teeth down through his gumshield and into his tongue, and this while Dave was wearing the big sixteen ounce gloves. A hard way to earn a living!

With preparations at an advanced stage for the journey to America, Dave and Arthur Boggis were invited to a luncheon hosted by Jack Solomons. All the boxing writers of the day were present but also in attendance was Bud Flanagan. Each guest was handed small artificial loaves with an inscription reading, 'Don't just say 'Brown' say 'Charnley'', an obvious reference to the type of bread. Solomons also presented a lucky silver horseshoe on a wooden base as a mascot to Dave on behalf of the Boxing Writers Club.

It's difficult to imagine nowadays how all the arrangements were made both for the journey to the fight location in Houston and the necessary accommodation for a training camp. Boggis was helped in this regard by one of his Kensington tenants, a Texan called Young, who had connections in Galveston.

As is still the case when fighters travel abroad the host promoter provides an allowance for the boxer and his entourage. Boggis was advised that a total of four people could be accommodated. Usually it would be expected that the boxer, his manager, the trainer and perhaps a regular sparring partner would go, however, Dave really didn't have a trainer as such and sparring partners had been arranged for him in America. So, on the journey with Dave and Boggis went younger brother Joe and, again demonstrating his continuing influence, Ray Bartlett.

The group left London Airport, now Heathrow, on a British Overseas Airways Corporation aircraft powered by four propellers! The flight was bound for New York but the first stage was a fourteen hour journey to a re-fuelling stop in Gandor, Newfoundland. Fortunately for Dave, the Captain, on learning he had a famous boxer on board, allowed him to sleep for part of the journey in a makeshift bed within the cockpit. When the passengers disembarked at Gandor they had to go upstairs on an elevator to the lounge area. When Joe and Dave were on it they looked down and saw the inscription 'J and E Halls, Dartford', where their father worked as an engineer!

This arduous journey then moved on to the second stage, New York's Idlewild Airport, now JFK. This time they met a reception committee and were whisked off to a restaurant in downtown Manhattan to meet the American boxing press to help publicise the forthcoming world title confrontation.

How exhausted they all must have been when they eventually arrived in Houston only to be met by the local mayor supported by a majorette style band. They were then taken to their base at the famous Rice Hotel in the centre of the city.

Angelo Dundee had organised the training facilities at Roxy's gym, a short walk from the hotel, and also engaged a series of sparring partners including Ernie Tubbs, Ray Portilla and two Salazar brothers. Also training in the gym was the heavyweight, Cleveland Williams, in preparation for a fight with Sonny Liston.

Although the locals thought that the weather was chilly,

particularly Cleveland Williams because he turned up at the gym wearing a heavy coat, the Londoners certainly didn't feel that way and Dave and Joe recall the gym feeling like a sauna. The sparring partners were excellent and always fought as suggested by Boggis and Bartlett. Within a few days however Dave began to feel uncomfortable with staying in the hotel. Being central, it was noisy at night and in the mornings Dave felt awkward arriving back at a *posh* hotel covered in sweat after his runs. Very quickly alternative accommodation was found at a nice house in the Jackson Heights area of Houston close to the countryside. This was now ideal for Dave's early morning runs and with a car laid on for the group getting to the gym was not a problem.

They were well looked after by Brown's manager Lou Viscusi who in the evenings regularly took them to Guido's Restaurant where the chefs could cook the meals *English style* as Dave would say. Of course there was an obligation to *sell* the fight and several times Dave had to meet the media. On one such occasion the group visited a local radio station and afterwards they were invited to take away any LPs of their choosing. At another event outside Houston they were being hosted by people hoping to publicise the fight there when a local jeweller approached Dave and presented him with a gold wristwatch. Typically for Dave his first thoughts were in relation to the difficulties he would have declaring it to Customs officials when he arrived back in Britain!

At the house in Jackson Heights Dave had two surprise visitors. Firstly a man originally from Peckham in London arrived and gave Dave a gift of English teabags a gesture he thought would make them feel more at home. But a bigger surprise appeared in the shape of cousin Jimmy Ralston who had travelled on his own all the way to Texas from Craigneuk. He was welcomed with open arms and stayed with them until the fight. Jimmy had said to his wife that he didn't want to miss seeing Dave in his biggest fight, and she encouraged him to go. He emptied the family Post Office account and travelled all the way by himself – an amazing commitment way back in 1959.

As fight time approached Dave and his manager were very pleased with their preparations and the only minor hiccup was a black eye Dave received in sparring with Tubbs. This did raise an issue with Arthur Boggis however as he had no recognised cut-man. He firstly asked Ray Bartlett if he would take on this responsibility but understandably he refused.

A few days before the fight Ruth and Boggis's partner Madelaine Wood arrived in Houston, and they were warmly welcomed. Around the same time the British boxing press made their appearance, including Frank Butler of the News of the World, Peter Wilson of the Daily Mirror, Harry Carpenter of the Daily Mail, George Whiting of the Evening Guardian, Tom Phillips of the Daily Herald and of course Reg Gutteridge of the Evening News.

In the immediate build up to the fight the American press predicted an easy victory for the champion who himself forecast a stoppage before the 7th round. Their British counterparts also favoured the American and both these views were reflected by the bookmakers odds. In the States Brown was 12-5 on while in Britain he was 3-2 on.

On the day of the fight, 2 December, Boggis eventually

found a local man, Perry Payne, to work in Dave's corner to deal with any cuts, a factor which could have been very important indeed. It is amazing that with the number of cuts Dave had received in his career to that date such an important consideration had not been decided until that late hour. At a very subdued weigh-in Dave sat in a chair with his arms folded and eyes closed waiting for the arrival of the champion. When he came in Brown looked the part, wearing a Stetson, sucking a toothpick and wearing cowboy boots. Dave weighed 9st 7lb 12oz with Brown four ounces heavier.

In America fights were scored by the referee supported by two ringside judges. For this fight the referee was Jimmy Webb and the judges were Ernie Taylor and Bill Cornelius. When Dave approached the ring in the Houston Coliseum he was preceeded by a Marine Corps guard of honour led by a Coventry born Sergeant, Sam Griffin. Nervous wife, Ruth, had to be moved from her seat at ringside and joined the British press contingent because her original view was blocked.

Ring announcer, Bill Whitmore called out the names, their records, and raised the anticipation in the unusually small crowd of 6,500. This was Dave's big chance, the day he had been waiting for since he first laced on the gloves at the Scout Hall in Little Queen Street. His biggest fans, dad William, brother of the same name and sister Isabel were sitting at home listening to the live radio broadcast and their nerves as the bell rang must have been at breaking point. Perhaps the calmest through all this would have been Dave himself simply because he always went into a fight thinking he would win.

In the 1st round both boxers were cautious and were quite

clearly sizing each other up. Brown was finding it easy to land with whiplash lefts and Dave's right eye began to redden. Dave's right leads were falling short and when he threw long lefts Brown blocked them before skipping away. Dave looked stiff and even perhaps overawed by the occasion. Brown came out for the 2nd and started to double up on the jab and throw over big right hands most falling short. Midway through the session the champion slammed his gloves together in apparent frustration but Charnley was not throwing anything in return. Charnley opened up a bit more in the 3rd but Brown was well in control and totally untroubled. In the next round Dave troubled Brown with a long left hook which knocked him back into the ropes but there was no follow up attack from the challenger. One of the judges scored this an even round. At the start of the 5th Dave came from his corner more like the fighter the British public had come to expect, moving forward, bobbing and weaving and stalking for an opening. Charnley shook Brown with a right hook, his best punch of the fight, and when he moved in again there was a flurry of punches from both boxers. Dave reeled back from this exchange obviously dazed and when the bell rang he staggered drunkenly back to his corner. Boggis saw a visibly swelling, split eyebrow, and when referee Webb approached the corner asking if the damage could be repaired, the manager sensibly answered in the negative. In that brief moment Dave's hopes, and indeed those of Arthur Boggis, had ended in a most unsatisfactory manner. Two out of three judges had awarded Charnley the last round.

Afterwards all of the American press corps claimed that a Brown right uppercut had caused the damage, while their

British counterparts generally felt that it had been a head clash. Dave has absolutely no doubts that the cut was caused by Brown's head although he accepts that it was unintentional. Brown was less than gracious when interviewed after the fight claiming that it was easy and that having trained so hard he now wanted another fight before the end of the year. His trainer Bill Gore said that his man had harder sparring sessions. Meanwhile the British press saw a two inch cut above Dave's right eye and agreed that it was a fight ending injury. When Boggis tried to claim that he felt Dave was just coming into the fight the press disagreed and their telegraphed reports tended to suggest that Dave had been out of his depth.

The following night when the BBC showed the fight many fans were shocked to see that he had not been as outclassed as the newspaper reports had suggested. Indeed the following week when the Boxing News came out, they too felt that the ringside journalists were well off the mark.

With the reduced gate at the fight, Jack Solomons' prediction, when the fight was announced, that Dave would clear £7,500 turned out be an over-estimation. His purse subsequently proved to be £4,300, still his biggest to date, but little compensation for his loss.

Dave still has the gloves he wore that night but unsurprisingly they are hidden away in a cupboard. There is also an interesting tale about where his trunks went. A few months after the fight Dave began taking an interest in a young amateur boxer from Ireland, Peter Cheevers. Dave was coaching the lad from Tallaght near Dublin who had won the British schoolboys title twice, as well as the London ABA championship. As a gesture of support, Dave presented him with the trunks.

While Arthur Boggis and Ray Bartlett flew home together, Dave, Ruth and brother Joe made their way to aunt Jean Ralston's house in New Jersey for a brief visit to recuperate and relax before heading home, this time on a direct flight from Idlewild to London aboard a new Boeing 707 jet.

There is an interesting footnote to the Texas visit as recounted by journalist Norman Giller. 'I clearly remember him (Arthur Boggis) telling us a mind-blowing tale about his visit to Texas with Dave for the first world title challenge against Joe Brown. He told Tim, Ron and I that he was taken for a ride by four hoodlum-type characters, who made it clear to him that if Dave won there could be dire consequences. It just might have been that Arthur was trying to impress us with a fabricated story, but for all his faults I don't think he would have made up such a startling story. It's history how Dave lost after a butt opened a gash over his eye. I always wondered what might have happened had he landed one of his knockout combinations?'

With the year coming to an end on a sad note, Dave still managed to attend as special guest at Christmas parties. One of these was at the annual function organised by J and J Maybank(Strood) Ltd for 500 local children within the Drill Hall in Sidcup. The event which was filmed by the BBC showed Dave box 10 year old Terry Lidsey in a makeshift ring. Dave was stopped again inside the distance in his next fight, this time by Santa Claus who was about to distribute parcels to the children.

Over the course of 1959 Dave had added the British Empire title to his British crown and at the same time had earned himself £13,000 (or around £247,000 today).

Historical Note – 1959

Nottingham Forest beat Luton Town to win the FA cup.
BBC introduce their Juke Box Jury show presented by David Jacobs
The first Mini takes to the road.
First section of the M1 motorway opens between Watford and Rugby
Margaret Thatcher becomes an MP for the first time taking the Finchley seat.

CHAPTER 9

European Champion, then It Goes All Quiet

If your whole life's ambition was to climb Mount Everest and the attempt had to be aborted 100 feet from the top due to bad weather, how do you respond? Do you give up and concentrate on more mundane things or do you strive to get back up there? Fighting for a world boxing title is not Mount Everest but perhaps the emotions they stir are comparable. This seems to have been the challenge facing the 24 year old Charnley following the loss to Brown. In comparative terms, he was now a rich man, was fit and healthy, had a nice wife and home, was very popular with the public and still held both the British and British Empire lightweight titles. Did he really feel he could get back up to the summit, and more importantly, did he really want to?

Dave had been training almost daily for over eight years. He had suffered scar tissue over and around his right eye, had a painful right elbow and a left hand which seemed to be constantly swollen. However, the ambition still burned inside and the determination to succeed was as obvious as ever to those around him. His brother Joe feels to this day that on reflection the fight with Brown had come too soon for him and it is likely that even if the cut had not happened the much more experienced champion would have prevailed. Dave, as we might imagine, disputes that assertion even to this very day. He says that he felt confident of beating Brown from the moment he accepted the fight.

Meanwhile another former opponent Carlos Ortiz had moved up to the newly created light-welterweight division and was generally accepted as the world champion in that category. Brown obviously was still champion at the lower weight but a close relationship had been struck between Jack Solomons and Brown's manager, Lou Viscusi, as well as with Ortiz's handlers which could encourage both groups to bring their fighters to London for a re-matches.

So, there were still opportunities on the horizon as the 1960s opened up. It should not be forgotten that there was a European title opportunity available if manager Boggis wanted to take that route. The Italian Mario Vecchiatto had won the vacant title from Frenchman Lahouari Godih in Milan by eighth round disqualification on 24 October and was scheduled to defend against Frenchman Saveur Benamou.

Nevertheless Jack Solomons had a fight date at the Empire Pool scheduled for 23 February and he needed a quality opponent for his main attraction. Having just fought for a world title he had to choose an opponent for Dave who would befit his status as a leading world title challenger. That man happened to be Vecchiatto's challenger, Benamou. He was the French champion and a Sephardi Jew, meaning that he was descendent from Spanish-Portuguese stock, but born in Algeria. Using his purses from boxing, Benamou had invested in a prosperous tailoring business in Paris which he ran with his wife. He had fought 27 times as a professional winning on 24 occasions.

Benamou had won the French title from Fernand Nollet and this earned him the nomination from the European Boxing Union to fight Vecchiatto.

The world rankings were released towards the end of January and they showed that Dave was still the number three contender for Brown's throne, with Paolo Rosi and Carlos Ortiz (even though he was fighting at 10st now) above him. European champion Mario Vecchiatto was placed at number nine.

The Charnley preparations took a severe jolt on 17 February when his house was burgled while he and his wife were out for the evening. Ruth had her engagement ring and other jewellery, valued in excess of £600, stolen. On the day before the fight Dave admitted to reporter Desmond Hackett that he had lost sleep over the theft and couldn't settle during the night.

It was business as usual on the evening of the fight with Dave's loyal fans packing the Empire Pool and cheering him to the rafters as he made his way to the ringside. Joe Charnley, now 20 years old, remembers going into Dave's dressing room before the fight and finding Dave as usual half-sleeping on the treatment table. When one of the ring whips arrived to tell Dave he was due to go on Joe recalls Dave saying that he hated this part of fighting at Wembley. At that time the dressing rooms were situated in a part of the stadium which meant the fighters had to enter onto a passageway and briefly walk through fans at the public bars before arriving at the stairway taking them to the ringside. Joe knew immediately what his brother meant. He was extremely uncomfortable with all the cheering and back-slapping he knew would take place before he reached the protected stairway because of his inherent shyness. Joe, on the other hand, confesses that he simply revelled in the adulation for his older brother and it made him feel ten foot tall.

The fight turned out to be just the test Charnley needed after the Brown defeat. Benamou turned out to be a game, strong and dangerous opponent who forced the best out of the British champion. As had become the norm in recent fights, Dave started slowly and seemed to some at ringside to be *gun-shy*. Benamou snatched the initiative in the first few rounds but after this Dave started to find his feet. He began to pick off the long right hands that the Frenchman was now throwing continuously and was retaliating with left hooks which were having an effect. Now warming to the task Charnley battered the Frenchman all over the ring drawing blood from his nose. The crown began to realise the *old* Charnley was now in full swing and the atmosphere inside the arena was electric. Over the last few rounds Dave confirmed his superiority without ever being in danger of stopping his opponent. At the end of fight, referee, Jack Hart had no hesitation in raising the hand of the Dartford man. Once again he had suffered a large swelling over his right eye and hung over the ropes for a rest indicating how tired he was at the finish up.

In the programme for the fight Jack Solomons had already indicated that the Empire Pool had been booked for another night of boxing only five weeks later, and it quickly became apparent that Dave was to top the bill again. This time he would have the chance to add a third title to his existing honours with the European championship up for grabs. His opponent would be the Italian holder, Mario Vecchiatto.

Vecchiatto, from Udine, was a top rate performer and was

certainly world class. He was 28 years old and had won 48 of 58 contests with only four defeats. As well as being the European champion, with his victory over Godih, he also held his national title, winning it eighteen months previously. He had fought to a fifteen round draw with Duilio Loi, then the holder, for the continental title just after annexing his Italian championship. At that time Loi was the number one contender for Brown's world crown. That same year Vecchiatto had beaten Orlando Zulueta just a year after he had challenged Brown in a world title fight. Their only common foe was Belgian Joe Woussen. Dave had stopped Woussen in the 10th round in 1957 and the following year Vecchiatto had beaten him on points.

At the weigh-in during lunchtime on the day of the fight, held as usual at Solomons gym, there was a surprise when Charnley came in four ounces over the limit. This was totally unexpected because, as had become the norm, Dave had went to the special scales at Jack Moffat's greyhound track in Crayford with brother Joe and had weighed in on the button. Perplexed, Dave went away briefly doing some skipping in the adjacent gym and came back now two ounces under the limit.

During the build up Boggis had been telling the press that Dave had become a more cultured performer, so the large capacity crowd which rolled up at Wembley were not sure what to expect. This may have been an explanation for the slow start Charnley made because some of the newspapermen had him losing all of the first four rounds. During this period he was caught regularly by right hooks from the Italian champion. Unusually for a big title fight the Belgian referee Phillipe De Backer noticed that both boxers were wearing black shorts so

Dave as the challenger had to put on navy blue ones at the end of the 1st round! The fight was not proving as exciting as the large crowd anticipated due to the many clinches the fighters got into and referee De Backer kept breaking them up in an effort to keep the fight flowing. At long last the Charnley fans had something to cheer when in the 5th their man landed with a right to the jaw which made Vecchiatto back off. Dave followed up with two further right hands but in his desperation he slipped and fell to the canvas allowing the champion to re-group. Although Charnley clearly won the round, Vecchiatto came back strongly in the next and following another clinch Dave emerged with a cut near his right eye. Charnley was now in full swing however and appeared to win both the 8th and 9th rounds with good solid scoring shots.

The referee was later to confirm that at the end of these nine rounds he had the fight even. Immediately the bell rang to open the 10th round Dave was on to the champion and landed a vicious right hook to the jaw as his opponent was moving forward. This caused a double impact and Vecchiatto fell face first onto the canvas. He jumped up at a count of six, but the referee, complying with European, but not British rules at the time, gave him a standing eight count before allowing Charnley to continue. It was clear Vecchiatto was badly hurt as he stood facing the crowd holding the top rope as the referee counted. Dave was onto him in a flash determined to end matters and chased his foe across the ring landing a right, a left, and a final right, which had Vecchiatto staggering backwards before slumping down on his hands and knees. He straightened his legs immediately but his gloves were still touching the canvas.

When he stood up he raised his arm and the referee took this as a sign of surrender, waving the fight off, giving the European championship to Dave. There was much controversy afterwards when the Italian camp claimed that their man was only signalling to the referee that as he had suffered a knockdown he was indicating his intention to take an eight count before carrying on. These were indeed the rules in continental Europe. However, when the referee was interviewed afterwards he stated 'When Vecchiatto raised his hand at the count of four I took it that he wanted to retire. The counts had been nine, and four, and I made the fighters dead level when the contest ended. Whatever Vecchiatto says now, as far as I am concerned he signalled his retirement.' Promoter Jack Solomons was unable to comment on the ending because he missed it, having been taken home after feeling ill. So, the Dartford Destroyer was now a triple champion and had earned £5,000 for his troubles. Incidentally he still has the crimson gloves he wore that night.

In the weeks following the fight Arthur Boggis revealed that he had made a gentleman's agreement with Saveur Benamou's manager which allowed the Vecchiatto fight to take place. Benamou had been the mandatory challenger but had stepped aside on the promise that, should Charnley win, his first defence would be against Benamou in Paris. At the same time, Solomons now fully recovered, was making bold statements indicating that he was actively seeking re-matches for Dave against either Brown or Ortiz.

As a forerunner to the differences which would later emerge in Dave's relationship with Boggis, the entrepreneurial meat trader encouraged Dave to endorse a new *Tubby* aerial for use in the home by the growing number of households owning a television set. Dave was pictured in the national press showing off the aerial which was claimed to be more efficient at receiving signals than the larger outdoor version. It was alleged that Boggis and Dave had formed a company to market the product. Some weeks later the Sunday Pictorial published an article which totally humiliated Boggis. The new company had claimed that their aerial was a miniature wonder and cost only thirty shillings. It was further asserted that the 'precision engineered instrument' was 'derived from the latest advances in electronics'. However investigators discovered it consisted of nothing more than eight feet of cheap wire, a plug, a plastic case, a rubber sucker and a three inch spring. The technical head of a large radio and television retailer examined it and declared the device was simply rubbish and was worth little more than two shillings. When Boggis was challenged on these findings he said that the engineer was only saying this due to 'sour grapes'. He added that the television trade were mad at him because his aerial showed them up for fitting expensive outside aerials when they were not needed. The Sunday Pictorial then bought a piece of wire and a plug for one shilling and tested the reception on Boggis's own television set using the wire as an aerial. There was no difference in quality of reception between the *Tubby* aerial and the cheap wire they had bought. The brazen Arthur stuck to his guns and said that his aerial did work and that it was still cheaper than the normal trade aerials. He added that he didn't know anything about the technical side of it and that he didn't really know himself how it worked!

Back on the boxing front Boggis had persuaded Benamou's team to accept a delay to a European title defence until the late summer. While Jack Solomons was still trying to negotiate a match with either Brown or Ortiz, he had succeeded in matching Dave with another American, Paul Armstead, on his Eve of the Derby show at Wembley.

The American was 23 years old, and although born in Texas, now lived permanently in Los Angeles. He was ranked number six in the world and had engaged in 37 fights, winning 28 and losing 8. He was the Californian lightweight champion and ranked sixth in the world. The only common foe with Charnley was Johnny Gonsalves. Armstead had beaten and lost to his fellow Californian in 1958.

In the lead up to the fight Arthur Boggis had to once again ask the Benamou camp to be patient and promised that Dave would go to Paris on 20 June to put his European title on the line. Subsequent events demonstrate that this was never going to happen. Boggis also bristled when commentators were suggesting that Dave never really shone nowadays in non-title fights. The manager explained that his charge had taken part in over 50 rounds of sparring, with, among others, George Cottle. George, a lifelong friend of Dave, was a good quality welterweight from Bermondsey who won 18 of 23 professional contest and was a regular and capable sparring partner.

Once again the large Charnley following made their way to Wembley on 31 May for Solomons Eve of the Derby show, and as expected, it was a sell out. At the start of the bout Dave boxed cautiously, similar to his performance against Vecchiatto. Many spectators, and reporters at ringside, bred on his exciting, aggressive style in his younger days saw this as an early sign of a decline. In actual fact, it seems more likely that it was an indication of a growing tactical maturity in terms of pacing himself for the longer distance fights against better opposition. Charnley, it has to be remembered, was still only 24 years old and approaching his prime as a boxer.

For the first three rounds Dave was content to jab consistently, and although perhaps a bit boring for the large crowd, it nevertheless built up a points lead. In the 4th round his tactics changed and he switched his attacks to the body. Three lefts sunk into the ribs of Armstead, but this had the effect of bringing the American's head down and into Charnley's, earning himself a warning. In the 5th Armstead mounted a comeback and towards the end of the round he landed with three right hands in succession. Dave pressed forward in the 6th and in the following round Armstead seemed to be coming on even though he received a minor cut. The 8th was an exciting round as both boxers stood toe to toe but there was no indication of the dramatic ending about to unfold.

At the start of the 9th both came out looking to take control but Charnley appeared to be taking the initiative with short right hooks. Peter Wilson of the Daily Mirror best described the surprise ending. 'Then all at once it was as though a grenade had been fused and the pin pulled out. From nowhere the two men rushed together all thoughts of defence forgotten and rained punches on each other's jaws. Both of them appeared to be landing solidly but finally a right hander from Charnley following a left uppercut sent Armstead tottering back and on to the canvas. Referee Andrew Smyth emotionlessly tolled off the seconds over Armstead's bowed back. The American squirmed around on his hands and knees like a sailor reluctantly swabbing the decks. Armstead seemed to be trying to position himself so that he could look at his corner and get a signal when to rise. In fact he ended with his back turned to the corner and he wasn't even properly in the act of rising at the time Smyth had got to ten.'

They don't write it like that now, do they? Afterwards Armstead said that he had never been hit as hard, and Dave added that when he landed the knockout punch he could feel the impact right up into his shoulder.

Before Dave left with wife Ruth on 7 June for a few weeks holiday in the summer sunshine of Juan les Pins on the French Riviera, Boggis was telling the press that there could be two other fights for Dave in 1960. He intended meeting with Benamou's manager, Gilbert Benaim, on 2 June with a view to arranging a title defence in July and then meeting Brown in London during September. Dave recalls that even in the lap of luxury among the new *jet set* in southern France he still could not get his training regime out his system. He would be up and out running every morning before the sun got up.

On return from holiday Dave and Ruth were invited to present prizes at the gala and sports day of Oakfield County Primary School in Dartford. The headmaster, a Mr Curwen, was Dave's former house master at Dartford East Secondary school. The gala was in aid of funds for a swimming pool with filtering plant for the school. The cost of the project was £1,200 which again tends to draw a comparison with Dave's purses.

There then followed a series of confusing events which would affect the timing of Dave's return to the ring. On 19 July, contrary to promises Boggis made to the Benamou people, he was scheduled to fight on a Stan Baker promotion at Streatham Ice rink against the South African Johnny Van Rensburg. Charnley had apparently contracted the flu and Stan Baker suggested a short postponement. Boggis brought in Doctors who said that this was not an option because Dave was too ill to train. Strangely enough this provoked Stan Baker along with Boxing Board secretary Teddy Waltham to visit the Charnley home. This seems to suggest that they thought Dave was not as ill as Boggis was suggesting. Dave remembers this unusual visit and at the time he was puzzled to find both men at his door. Dave strongly maintains that he never pulled out of a fight feigning injury or illness and indeed claims the exact opposite pointing out he went through with fights when he wasn't fit. Dave as always let his manager do all the negotiating and was never involved in discussions with other managers or even promoters, but as he got older, and perhaps wiser, he did start to wonder what Boggis was saying and doing behind the scenes. Regardless, this fight was re-scheduled for 23 August.

Unfortunately, that bill also fell through, so Stan Baker and Boggis agreed that Dave would eventually fight at Streatham Ice Rink on 8 November against the Spaniard, Bobby Ros. Stan Baker's frustration must have been evident when towards the end of October Dave broke his left hand on the solid head of Nigerian sparring partner, Junior Cassidy, at the Thomas à Beckett causing a November cancellation. In the meantime problems were mounting for Boggis and Dave, when Mickey Duff, having won the purse bids to stage Dave's mandatory defence of the European title against Benamou, lodged an official protest with the Boxing Board.

On 28 October in Los Angeles Joe Brown retained his world title for the ninth time by outpointing Cisco Andrade over fifteen rounds.

The year was ending with Dave being inactive for the longest period since he took up boxing almost thirteen years previously. Illness and a broken hand were the principal causes but it has to be said that Boggis's manoeuvring was starting to have an adverse effect on his protégés career. The year of course had not been all bad news. The European crown was secured and his world ranking had improved. His earnings would probably have been in excess of £10,000 and when you consider that this would have bought eight swimming pools for Oakfield Primary school Dave was still doing OK thank you very much! His ring performances had become better paced and the punching power was still a factor in his favour.

It is worth examining how Dave's style of fighting had developed. Remember that he was a southpaw, with his right hand and right foot being in front. It is often the case that southpaws, with their stronger left hand, would neglect the other mitt possibly due to it being weaker. What many people did not realise however was that Dave was naturally right handed. So, with his stronger right hand, he would often catch skilful and experienced opponents as they came in, with a powerful right hook, and this would happen time and time again during fights. When looking at old films of these fights it becomes obvious what was happening, and yet Dave's opponents still got caught repeatedly with the same punch.

The following year would be the pinnacle of Dave's boxing career so perhaps the long lay-off in 1960 helped that to happen?

Historical Note – 1960
Prince Andrew born
Cyprus gains independence from Britain
Beatles perform for the first time in Hamburg
Francis Chichester sails solo across the Atlantic in 40 days.
The first episode of Coronation Street is shown
Wolves win the FA cup with a victory over Blackburn Rovers
Manchester City pay a record fee of £55,000 to Huddersfield Town for Denis Law.

CHAPTER 10

Second World Title Challenge

After such an uncertain year during which illness and hand injuries had scuppered planned contests, 1961 proved to be completely different. For a top level triple champion it seems amazing nowadays to comprehend the fact that Dave was to fight on seven occasions, all of them against quality opposition. He would fight for the world title, defend his European championship on three occasions, at long last defend his British crown, and in addition box against three top level Americans. He would fight on the continent for the first time and have two fights within seven days of each other. These fights would have grossed approximately £400,000 at today's value with, of course, Arthur Boggis claiming his 25% managers cut. In the autumn Dave would branch out into a completely knew and unexpected line of work which would startle the hard bitten boxing press corps and provide plenty of column inches.

At the start of the year it was clear that Stan Baker held an enforceable contract to promote Dave's next fight at Streatham Ice Rink. Boggis was intent on ensuring that Dave had a worthwhile opponent, so acting on this, Baker bought out the contract for the European title defence against Benamou from Mickey Duff. The fight was scheduled for 17 January but disaster was awaiting the unlucky promoter. On a visit to Paris to finalise the arrangements with the Benamou people Baker received a telephone call in his hotel room advising him that Benamou had been suspended by the French boxing federation. When the news reached Boggis he told Baker that he would not be as fussy as he had been previously with regard to choices of opponent as long as Dave's seven and a half months absence from the ring was brought to an end.

After several frantic transatlantic phone calls Stan managed to secure the services of the number seven ranked fighter, Gene Gresham. The American had been born in Lafayette, Alabama but was now based in Detroit. He was only 22 years old but had engaged in 31 fights winning 28 and drawing 1. The only common opponent had been Paul Armstead. Gresham had beaten him on a ten rounds points decision only nine months previously. Of further interest was the fact that Gresham had beaten Laouari Godih in September 1960, the man Vecchiatto had narrowly beaten to win the European title. So, the substitute opponent was probably a more capable fighter than the first choice – Benamou.

Two ringside reporters, Ron Mackenzie and Joe Bromley, showed their insight and detailed knowledge of the sport by identifying just how great a fighter Charnley had become. They could not have known just how successful, in almost all aspects, this year would be for Charnley when they covered the Gresham fight in the middle of January. Both wrote in glowing terms about Dave's performance with Bromley's headline in particular stating 'CHARNLEY IS GREAT'.

Dave weighed in at 9st 11lb and the referee was Tommy Little. At the start the American seemed to be setting the pace but was unsettled by Dave's southpaw stance. After a quiet first three rounds Dave opened up in the 4th and had Gresham momentarily hanging onto the ropes from a series of murderous right hooks. In the next round Gresham was in trouble again from a Charnley right-hander. It was all Charnley and most thought he won every round. In the last round Gresham's resistance finally gave out when a short right hook sent him down, clinging to Charnley as he went pulling the home fighter onto the canvas with him. Referee Little counted to five before Gresham got to his feet. When the final bell rang the referee had no hesitation in raising Charnley's arm. Afterwards Dave mentioned that he had to be careful to avoid any more cut eyes which could jeopardise future fights and Gresham graciously conceded that Charnley was surely one of the best lightweights in the world. He added that the Charnley right hook was 'sheer murder!'.

Just over four weeks later Stan Baker promoted Dave again at Streatham Ice Rink this time with his European title on the line. His opponent by way of Martinique, but now a French citizen, was Fernand Nollet.

Nollet was 29 years of age and was the current French champion. He'd had 54 fights, winning 35 and losing only 7. He had the proud distinction of never having being knocked off his feet during a fight. Dave and Nollet had seven common opponents. Like Dave, Nollet had beaten Woussem, Coppens and Willie Lloyd but he had went one better, because he had actually beaten Guy Gracia. He had drawn and lost to Vecchiatto, drawn with Spider Kelly and been beaten by Willie Toweel.

The fight on 21 February turned out to be a tough, gruelling fifteen rounds battle. An estimated 800 fans from Dartford and Bexley made their way on this Tuesday night and helped fill the venue to capacity. Unusually Dave started well and appeared to take the first three rounds fairly comfortably with a point scoring right jab. At the same time he seemed to be open for long right hand swings to the body from the Frenchman which seemed to take effect later on in the fight. Heads were clashing with Charnley equally at fault. In the middle rounds Nollet began to come more into the fight using long right hands and a stabbing left jab. As the fight progressed through the 10th round Charnley appeared to be losing steam and seemed happy to clinch and hold on whenever he got the chance. By the 13th round some of the crowd were getting restless mostly due to the lack of fireworks but also because they sensed that Nollet was closing the gap on Charnley's early lead. But all that was to change. Once again Nollet caught Dave with his head on the eyebrow which had caused the problem in the Brown fight. The wound opened quickly and the blood flowed freely down Charnley's face. The crowd and ringside reporters feared the worst. The injury however had the opposite effect on the champion and breathed life into his tiring frame. His corner patched the eye up between rounds and in the 14th and 15th he stormed after Nollet. With about a minute to go Charnley landed the punch of the night, a right hook which caused the Frenchman's legs to sag. Dave chased after Nollet with the crowd on their feet and the final bell did not come soon enough as far as the challenger was concerned. As Nollet staggered back to his corner Dutch referee Ben Bril raised Charnley's arm in victory.

As Dave left the ring he was clearly in distress and had to be supported by his cornermen as he made his way back to the dressing room. Once inside he was sick and exhausted. When the press were allowed in for their interviews Dave sat on the treatment table with his head bowed. He claimed that the heat in the hall plus the smoky atmosphere had caused him to be unwell but some journalists felt it was more due to the body punches of Nollet. Boggis was adamant that the cut eye would not jeopardise the proposed world title challenge to Joe Brown now being mooted for April. Dr Saville, the Board doctor recommended that the eye injury be stitched and indicated that it should heal within two months. Days after the fight Dave and Ruth left London Airport for a well earned two weeks holiday to Nice.

The scene was set for Dave's second attempt to wrest the world title from Joe Brown, with the date now confirmed for 18 April at Earls Court in London. In order to get the fight Boggis had to agree that in the event of a Charnley victory his man would grant Brown a re-match in Houston within 90 days. Such a deal was frowned on by the British Boxing Board but in Texas the boxing authorities there actually insisted on a return clause. To get over this hurdle documents were lodged with the Board seeking approval for Dave to travel to Texas to fight Brown by the end of July seemingly ignoring the fact that there was to be a fight in April. Simultaneously Brown's manager lodged a similar request with the Texas commission, so both parties were now appeased.

In 2009 British boxing journal, the Boxing News, reached their century of publication and produced a large glossy magazine in commemoration. A section within claimed that the 'golden age' for boxing worldwide was between 1940 and 1969. Using all the magazine's resources they conducted a poll to decide who the top ten boxers were from that era. 'Old Bones' Joe Brown didn't get a mention! This was sad but understandable. Brown was not a flamboyant media personality nor was he based in those major boxing cities of New York, Philadelphia, Chicago, Los Angeles or San Francisco. He was from Baton Rouge, Louisiana fighting out of New Orleans and then Houston, Texas. Perhaps the Boxing News pollsters should have looked a bit more closely at the Brown record.

Since winning the title in August 1956 he had defended it successfully nine times. That averages out at a championship defence every six months for four and a half years against all the main contenders. As if that was not enough, in between those defences he had another SIXTEEN fights, winning eleven, losing three and drawing two. He was a classical boxer. Great left jab and right cross. He could hook in close with either hand, and most importantly, due to the experience gained from over 100 fights, he knew how to control a fight. This meant he could dictate the pace, he could dominate from the centre of the ring and make the other fighter do all the work from the outside. He was not a one-punch knockout artist, another reason why he might not have reached the higher echelons, but he could punch with authority. An opponent could not afford to simply disregard their defence to get close to Brown because he could cause damage. This was what the Dartford Destroyer was up against.

Dave's preparations could not have been better. His training sessions at the Thomas à Beckett were well attended by sports fans and journalists alike. His chief sparring partner was Frenchman Sauveur Chiocca, supported by the ever reliable George Cottle and amateur star, Larry O'Connell. Chiocca was a fully blown welterweight who had fought all over the world and had tried three times to win the French title. Larry O'Connell, an amateur internationalist at the time, would later become one of Britain's top quality Star Grade referees officiating at world title fights all over the globe. Larry was brought in because he was a tall, fast, orthodox boxer who could reflect the style expected from Brown. Larry tells a humorous tale from one such sparring session. As the fight was approaching, Larry made his way at lunchtime to the Beckett from his job as an engraver with Cartiers for a few rounds of sparring with Dave. The press photographers were out in full force for their national newspapers, as the interest in the fight was reaching fever pitch. Knowing how Dave sparred, Larry was concentrating completely on the job in hand. So much so, that unusually for him, he landed a perfectly placed and forceful right cross on the Charnley chin, forgetting entirely that the world's boxing press were assembled. Larry remembers seeing an unfortunate (for him) change in the Charnley expression, and immediately realised he'd overstepped the mark. The Dartford Destroyer in Dave emerged and Larry was pummelled all over the ring until manager Boggis stepped into the ring and brought a premature end to the publicity show. No doubt the viewers thought this a typical stage managed production – but Larry knows differently!

Meanwhile the champion had arrived in the country on the 7 April and set up camp in the Army Training gym at the White

City where manager Lou Viscusi and trainer Billy De Foe supervised his work outs. Also with them to handle the press interest and to avoid too many distractions was Brown's publicity man, Frank Godoe.

There was not a single reporter in any of the national newspapers predicting a Charnley victory but it's unlikely that Dave would have been reading much as the fight approached. As had become normal in the build up to big fights Dave's brother Joe would move into his Bexley house basically to keep his mind occupied and to act as a buffer when the press and visitors came to the house. On the morning of the fight Joe and Dave walked as usual from Bexley to Crayford greyhound track and back to check on Mr Moffat's scales that he was within the limit. They were then given a lift to the weigh-in held as usual at Solomons gym in Windmill Street. They were dropped off in nearby Leicester Square and as they were walking in Shaftesbury Avenue they bumped into the well known singer Adam Faith who stopped to give Dave his best wishes for the fight. When they approached the gym they found hundreds of fans outside and a great cheer went up when they saw Dave. Once again at the weigh-in cousin Jimmy Ralston from Craigneuk, as he had done for the first fight in Texas, arrived unannounced along with another Craigneuk friend, Billy Reid. Billy was a professional footballer with Motherwell and had travelled down with the team to watch his team mates Ian St John and Bert McCann play for Scotland against England at Wembley taking the opportunity to slip away for the fight.

There were none of the modern day stare-downs, the fighters simply stood on the large coal mine type scales and had their weight confirmed by Boxing Board officials. A few photographs were taken and off went the respective camps to prepare for the fight. Dave and his group had to push their way through the throng outside and as expected there were lots of back- slapping and good luck wishes exchanged. Dave couldn't wait to get away but Joe remembers how proud he felt for his brother. The small group went to Braganza's restaurant in Frith Street, Soho, before moving on to Boggis's flat in Kensington where Dave had a sleep before the short car ride to Earls Court.

Back in Dartford and Bexley some 2,500 Charnley fans were embarking on buses, cars and taxis in expectation of witnessing their local lad winning the world title. They would have got reasonable odds at the bookmakers because they were quoting Brown as favourite at between 6-5 and 7-4 on. The Exhibition Hall at Earls Court was a huge arena for a boxing match but it was filled to its 18,000 capacity. If it was an intimidating atmosphere for the champion he didn't show it. He looked calm and assured as Johnny Best made the announcements. Dave stood resplendent in his lucky satin dressing gown, a gift from famous band leader and television star, Billy Cotton. Cotton had a famous catchphrase 'Wakey, Wakey' and when Dave first got the gown it was suggested that he should have this emblazoned on the back. There was no way Dave would contemplate this, however he had it stitched under the collar, and Cotton was tickled pink by this gesture.

Solomons had installed his old eighteen foot Harringay ring for the fight – a fact which didn't please Arthur Boggis. Dave's manager felt that the large ring would favour the champion. For the fight, unlike the first battle in Houston, the sole arbiter would be the English referee, Tommy Little. There were no judges.

Dave went straight into the attack in an effort to throw the champion out of his stride but Brown stuck out that left jab which scored repeatedly, bringing an early smudge over Dave's right eye. In the next round the crowd erupted when Brown wobbled into the ropes. Both then fell to the ground following a clinch as the tensions rose. Charnley continued to apply the pressure in the 3rd and 4th rounds and both fighters were warned by referee Little to watch their heads. In the 5th a short vicious right hand from Brown opened a bad cut on the bridge of Dave's nose, an injury which would continue bleeding for the remainder of the contest. Brown later alleged that this punch broke one of his knuckles. Nevertheless most observers still gave Dave this round and the next. After six rounds it seemed Dave was assuredly in front. The next round however clearly went to the champion who boxed superbly. Dave appeared to forget his gumshield at the start of the 8th but his left hooks to the body and short rights appeared to give him this round also. With the fight just over halfway complete it was very close, swinging firstly one way then the other, but the challenger seemed to be edging it. As the fight entered its last third Brown sensed that his title may be slipping and he stepped up a gear. During the next three rounds he jolted Dave's head back with powerful right hands and left jabs, probably swinging the fight back in his favour. Dave, however, could see the faint outline of the finishing tape and began to force the fight in the 13th. He had the huge crowd on their feet when he drove Brown to the ropes with body punches and caused a small cut over the champions eye. The Charnley attack carried on into the 14th round as he pummelled away at Brown, and when both fighters came out for the last everyone had to admit it was close. Harry Carpenter had the fight dead even. Donald Saunders at the Telegraph had Brown in front –just. The Boxing News correspondent thought the outcome hinged on the last round. Both fighters were visibly exhausted and their punches lacked power and were thrown clumsily, however the forward motion and aggression by Charnley clearly won him the last round.

Boggis and his cornermen were up on the ring apron ready to lift the new world champion when referee Little strode over to Brown's corner and raised his arm in victory. All hell broke loose. Programmes were thrown into the ring and the crowd turned nasty. Referee Little was quickly ushered out of the ring under a police escort, and so disgusted with the decision, the Boxing News corresponded felt like joining in the melee. The ring whip quickly got the next contestants into the ring but even when their names were announced the crowd continued to jeer and stamp their feet.

The fight was close, that was not in doubt. Those at ringside were obviously rooting for a Charnley victory, and even the reliable Boxing News had a vested interest in Britain claiming a world title. But what galled most people was the fact that anywhere else in the world, in such circumstances, the home based referee would have awarded the decision to the local fighter. That shouldn't be the case, but it was then, and still is today even with three ringside judges. What is important was the fact that the following morning when the national newspapers hit the stands only one ringside reporter gave Dave the fight – Harry Carpenter. Donald Saunders scored it by one round to Brown but others had the champion retaining by nine rounds to three, with three scored even. The bottom line was that the result was in the record books and Brown still held the title.

Dave was reported to have earned £10,000 from the fight while Brown took home £18,000. At the end of the year the American based boxing monthly *The Ring*, edited by the influential Nat Fleischer, voted this fight the best of 1961. This was of little consequence to Dave and his team.

CHAPTER 11

Hammering Opponents and Hairdressing

We should be entitled to think that a boxer having fought fifteen hard rounds for the world title would not be required to defend his European championship a month later. But Dave had been contracted to fight Italian champion, Giordano Campari, in Italy on 18 May. Arthur Boggis was aptly named because the mind *boggles* with how he could possibly have agreed to such a venture so soon after Dave's tangle with Joe Brown. Thankfully for all concerned this date was cancelled when Dave tore a muscle in his right calf and a new date and new opponent arranged. This fuelled the speculation amongst Boxing Board officials that Dave seemed to get ill or suffer injuries when either a fight or the money wasn't to his liking. Again, it has to be said that Dave emphatically denies this ever happened.

Dave did defend the continental crown on 5 July in Rome against Raimondo Nobile. Before this however, Dave and Ruth went off to the French Riviera for a well deserved months rest and recuperation. When Dave got home around the middle of June he learned that the fight was to take place at the outdoor Flaminio Stadium and that a large hostile crowd would await his arrival. Already the British sports journalists were comparing his chances with those of the Roman gladiators, drawing on their past experiences when British boxers had fought in that country. Given the large number of reporters from London who actually attended the fight there can be little doubt there was also a lot of champagne corks popping at the thought of a nice little paid holiday in Rome during July. Or is that a bit harsh?

Dave and Ruth arrived at Rome Airport from London the day before the fight amid scenes reminiscent of welcoming royalty. All the other passengers were required to remain in their seats while Dave and Ruth went down the flight steps literally onto a red carpet. Italian officials presented Ruth with a large bouquet and they were then whisked passed immigration and customs controls.

Once the group settled in their hotel, Boggis emerged to meet with the British press. He expressed his fear of his fighter being *nobbled* so he said that he would supervise Dave's food intake and when they went to the stadium Boggis would take his own water, bucket and sponge. Boggis even suggested that he might move the camp to another hotel if he wasn't satisfied with arrangements. Soon after, Boggis ordered scales to be brought to their hotel and after the check weight was completed the hotel chef was woken from his afternoon siesta to prepare a steak for the fighter.

The little 24 year old Sicilian had an outstanding fight record with 27 wins and only 1 defeat from 30 contests. His only loss was to the world featherweight champion, Davey Moore, and he was the current Italian featherweight champion. The words *little* and *featherweight* would have important consequences as the fight unfolded. Nobile and his family had based themselves up in Mount Ombraro in the Apennines and according to local reports he was working his way through a host of southpaw sparring partners. Ex-champion, and occasionally Dave's trainer in past times, Dave Crowley, who now owned a bar in the Via Aurora met Dave and Boggis at their hotel and advised them that the Italians, while supporting Nobile, were taking bets at 3-1 against a Nobile victory. Hardly an encouraging statistic on a two horse race!

The entire day of the fight turned into a bit of a shambles. The first indication that it was going to be one of those days was at the afternoon weigh-in. Looking tanned and fit Dave stepped on the scales and found himself to be two ounces over the limit. Surprising given that he had weighed himself on scales at the hotel. Nevertheless he quickly walked off the excess in the ninety degree heat. Then it was on to the stadium for a scheduled 10.30pm start time.

When the 30,000 in attendance realised that the bout would not commence at that time they began to get restless and when Dave reached the ring thirty minutes short of midnight they were in a state of high agitation. This was exacerbated when the Italian challenger stepped into the ring fifteen minutes later without his hand bandages having been put on. Everybody, including Dave, had now to wait a further ten minutes while these were applied. This had undoubtedly all been stage managed in a futile attempt to unsettle the champion who was now more determined than ever to hand out a beating for such shabby treatment. Ringside reporters noted that as the bell approached Charnley had a nasty looking smirk on his face as a result of the Italian antics.

Among the British press in attendance were Donald Saunders, Gerard Walter, Reg Gutteridge, Harry Carpenter, Desmond Hackett, George Whiting, and the Boxing News correspondent. When both fighters came together Charnley appeared so much bigger and strangely for Dave, he was also taller. Dave was well and truly up for the task and moved straight into the attack with a left hook to the body and a right to the jaw. Moments later Nobile was on the floor when a right swing from Charnley appeared to catch him off balance. However this was a portent of things to come. Dave continued to score at will with body shots and a hard right drove the Italian onto the ropes. Nobile fought back in vain because just before the end of the 1st round Dave smashed home two hard rights which caused Nobile to stagger to the wrong corner when the bell went.

Nobile came out in a crouch for the start of the 2nd and he quickly walked onto three hard right hooks which brought up a swelling on his left cheek bone. Nobile was then battered around the ring and several times his legs buckled from the onslaught. By this point the British press had decided that the Italian was out of his depth. In the next round the hammering continued and this time Nobile had to take two counts as Dave tried to finish him off.

Swiss referee, Robert Seidel, had little to do up to this point but that would all change in the 4th. Charnley came out and caught Nobile with two quick right hands and then seemed to wrestle his opponent to the ground. Referee Seidel administered a severe lecture to the champion. Immediately Dave drove Nobile to the ropes and let go with everything he had. Nobile staggered along the ropes but bravely refused to go down. This was clearly a slaughter but the referee refused to intervene. Some of the spectators at ringside had seen enough and began to throw programmes and even a lighter into the ring. Then moments later, into the ring fluttered a towel, the traditional means a corner uses to surrender on behalf of their fighter. Referee Seidel believing, as did everyone else, that it had come from the Italians corner, stopped the fight. That's when all hell broke loose. The Italian corner men climbed into the ring and protested that they hadn't thrown in the towel. Boggis believing this was yet another trick by the Italians, entered the ring also and argued furiously with Seidel. While all this was going on Dave, fully aware of the state Nobile was in, was shouting for Boggis to let things be so he could get on and finish the job. The referee then went to consult officials at ringside who clearly instructed him to allow the fight to continue. Still Boggis protested and it was only when Seidel threatened to disqualify Charnley that he reluctantly went back onto the other side of the ropes. As we can imagine, during this minute or so interruption, Nobile was being revived by his corner and when the referee signalled for the fight to continue he was at least able to stand up unaided. The remainder of the momentous 4th somehow had only twelve seconds to run before the bell sounded. As Dave prepared to come out for the 5th the referee was called over to Nobile's corner where it was indicated that their man was retiring due to a damaged thumb. Dave simply stood in his corner and laughed at the farcical outcome.

Dave and Boggis were assured of receiving the £6,000 purse because the wily manager had insisted that the money be lodged in a bank before the fight commenced. Despite all the attempts at cheating the champion out of his title, the Italians still made approaches to Boggis to return to Italy to defend his crown against the Italian lightweight champion, Campari, offering £10,000 for the privilege. Dave and Ruth left all that behind as they flew directly back to Juan les Pains to pick up on the holiday they interrupted with preparations for the fight.

It is clear that the seven months rest during the second half of 1960 coupled with a training regime which now included rests between fights was proving beneficial. When he returned from Juan Les Pains Dave went straight back into training camp for a fight on 5 September against the number seven contender in the world, yet another American, Lennie Matthews.

It emphasizes just how highly Dave was rated at the time that this match, with a world title contender, was considered a routine, marking time sort of fight until he could get back into the ring with Joe Brown. Being a world ranked fighter didn't even begin to describe the quality of opposition Dave was about to face. The Philadelphia boxer, even though he was only 22 years of age, had been fighting the best lightweights in the world for the past two years with some considerable success. He had boxed four men who had fought, and lost, to Brown for the world title. He had knocked out Kenny Lane and Johnny Busso in the 3rd and 1st rounds respectively. He had also outpointed Orlando Zulueta, but lost to Paola Rosi. He had won and lost to former Charnley opponent, Paul Armstead, and outpointed Johnny Gonsalves. He had been knocked out by Carlos Ortiz and lost on points to Willie Toweel. Just for good measure he had twice outpointed former European title challenger Laouari Godih and all of these fights had happened in the last three years.

On the morning of this Harry Levene promotion at Wembley Reg Gutteridge considered this to be a *bread and butter* fight for Dave as he strove to keep in tune for a rumoured third battle with Joe Brown in January at Madison Square Garden in New York. Thankfully no one in the Charnley inner circle was taking Matthews lightly. It was becoming increasingly more difficult to predict how the early rounds of a Charnley fight would progress. On this particular night, however, he started like a steam train. He ripped combinations of punches into the Americans body, rocked him with jabs and hooks to the head, and completely threw him out of his stride. Matthews would later claim he hurt his right hand in the 1st round but as he threw it regularly thereafter this was simply taken as an excuse. For six rounds Dave kept up the pace while Matthews strove manfully, but in vain, to stem the tide. Some of his punches did land but Charnley kept coming.

Between the 7th and 9th rounds, seemingly well ahead, Dave slowed the pace and demonstrated excellent defensive skills, countering Matthews' attacks with accurate right hooks and the occasional burst of punches which drew applause from the capacity crowd. The usual last round slugfest that Dave normally produced did not materialise and he stood off and picked his punches, clearly hurting the visitor in the process. When the bell rang, Charnley confidently walked over to referee Eugene Henderson to have his arm raised. Some reporters the next day claimed that this had been Dave's greatest performance, so easily did he handle a world class opponent.

Following his world title challenge to Brown in April Dave and wife Ruth began making plans to secure their future after he had hung up the gloves. Dave had seen other fighters spend their hard earned purses as they went along with little thought as to how they would fund their life after their career came to an end. Dave was determined this would not happen to him.

However, the route he took was rather surprising for a boxer and of course the press made a meal of it. For some time Dave had marvelled at how costly Ruth's weekly hairdressing bill had become. He had inherited the ability to look after his money from his Scottish parents and thought to himself that here was a business he could get into. As was typical for Dave, he had to devote all his energies into any project in which he became involved. Accordingly, from June until December he took on an expensive hairdressing course in London each afternoon after his training had finished. Dave admits now that it was never his intention to actually do women's hair on a regular basis, he really just wanted to know all about the business. Dave then invested around £9,000 in buying premises in Spital Road, Dartford which he converted into a state of the art salon kitted out with all the most modern equipment. Dave remembers thinking at the time that the French owner of another hairdressing salon in the town must have hated the new competition, given that Dave's salon had double the number of hard drying machines.

Dave was starting to display the trappings of success his boxing career had provided. He had taken a liking to fashionable Italian clothes, and brother Joe remembers he had two sets of suits – one for when he was in training, because he would be thinner, and another set, in a size larger, when he became slightly heavier. He now had a pearl grey Jaguar with maroon leather upholstery, which became well known in the Dartford area.

On 28 October Joe Brown retained his world crown for the eleventh time with a points victory over Bert Somodio in the Phillipines.

While Dave had been winning and retaining the European title, fighting for the world championship as well tackling world ranked contenders, the British Boxing Board had forced through a series of elimination contests to decide who would be the next challenger for his British crown. It had been over four years since Dave had won the title from Joe Lucy and he had yet to defend it. The winner of this elimination competition was Welshman, David Hughes. Not many boxing fans from that time will recognise this name because the coloured fighter from Cardiff was known by everyone, with affection, as 'Darkie' Hughes. Of course, in modern society, such a nickname is unacceptable but in those unenlightened days that was the only name he was known by.

It has to be recognised that Dave, and Boggis, did not want this fight. It was forced on them by the Boxing Board of Control. They obviously had a wish to keep the lightweight title moving forward and were being pressured by Hughes' team to get Charnley into the ring. It is clear now that the Board must have threatened Boggis with stripping Dave of the British championship if he didn't comply. Maybe that was what was hoped for back in Cardiff. When purse bids were invited, only Reg King, a promoter from Nottingham, bothered to reply. He only bid £2,000 for the contest and with Dave's end as the champion being 60% of this figure, he stood to earn only

£1,200. It has to be remembered that it was expected that his European and Empire titles would also be on the line.

Weeks before the fight Reg Gutteridge saw the dangers. His headline in the Evening News and Star read 'BAN THIS FIGHT'. Gutteridge identified that Hughes hadn't fought for a year and was only a part-time professional working during the day as a turbine-fitter. Charnley was the number two lightweight in the world and in the form of his life.

So confident of a quick victory was Boggis that he had arranged a fight with another world ranked opponent just seven days afterwards. So on 20 November no one knows what was going through Hughes' mind when he stepped into the ring to face Charnley. Afterwards Dave said he was only concerned about winning and he thought he'd have to chase the challenger to do so.

Mickey Duff who was the matchmaker for Dave's next fight decided to drive up from London to spectate so he could learn at first hand if his proposed contest would be in any danger. Duff knew the fight was scheduled to start at 8.30pm and he turned up at the Ice Rink at that appointed time. He missed the entire contest which was not so surprising given that it went down in history as the shortest ever British title fight. Within forty seconds Hughes was down and out and worryingly did not regain consciousness for over a minute.

Dave came out his corner like a sprinter responding to the gun and landed a right hand which shocked the challenger. A further right and left bundled the Welshman halfway through the ropes. Hughes came out from the ropes, circled indecisively to his left and Dave pounced again, first missing with a right then landing with a right and left which put Hughes back into the ropes. Hughes sagged towards the floor and a short count was administered. The challenger heaved himself up. Dave had backed off but sprang in again with a full blooded right hand which caught Hughes on the side of the jaw. He spun round and crashed face down in his own corner. Hughes lay straight and still and had not moved by the time referee Frank Wilson completed the count. For several minutes afterwards there was an anxious huddle around the challenger but finally he was able to leave the ring on shaky legs. According to promoter King, Dave received £1,686 including television fees while the luckless Cardiff man acquired a painful £800. When Hughes hit the deck Dave's wife Ruth left her ringside seat and made for the dressing room area. She later admitted feeling sick at the outcome.

Dave had very little time to reflect on the merits of having to take part in such a mismatch because the very next morning he was back out pounding the streets near his home in Bexley. With an important fight in six days time there was no time for relaxation. His opponent was Langston Carl Morgan, or LC, as he preferred to call himself. Morgan, from Youngstown, Ohio, was a very experienced 27 year old who had engaged in 63 fights up till then. He had won 45, but his victory in September over Dave's mandatory opponent for the European title, Giordano Campari, had lifted him into the number nine spot in the world rankings. He arrived in Manchester a week before the fight and was cutting a swathe through his sparring partners. Observers noted an uncanny resemblance to Joe Brown.

This was to be Dave's first fight in Manchester for five years and promoter Harry Levene had high hopes of filling the Belle Vue arena. He would not be disappointed. Neither were the fans who turned up. Dave put on a master-class performance and convinced everyone, including Harry Levene, that he was the *real* world champion. The fight started in exciting fashion with both boxers standing toe to toe in the 1st round and ringside reporters felt that either man could win by a knockout, such was the punching power on display. Morgan was thought to have had just about the best of that round. He landed with a hard right hook to the head but Dave countered with his own right and the force of the blow turned Morgan halfway round. Near the end of the round Dave was caught by a right at close quarters and knocked back with a follow up right. Morgan opened up the 2nd with a left hook to the head and the skin around Charnley's eyes was looking raw. Dave started to score well to the body and the American was feeling the effects. In the 3rd, three right hooks to the chin spelt the finish for Morgan. The third right made the American bend at the knees and a following left to his face sent him down on his back. When the count reached eight he clawed his way off the canvas and was sagging into the ropes. He pulled himself upright but with his gloved hands still dangling by his waist referee Harry Humphries spread his arms wide to signal the end.

This brought the curtain down on a momentous year for Dave. He was widely regarded as the best lightweight in the world and was reckoned to have earned in excess of £20,000 throughout the year. A figure approaching £400,000 at today's value. Harry Levene was offering a lot of money to entice Brown back to Britain but at the same time Arthur Boggis was in negotiations with Italian promoters either to have Dave fight Duilio Loi for the newly created world junior welterweight title, or a European championship defence against Giordano Campari. It is likely that at this point Dave was in his fighting prime.

Historical Note – 1961
Avengers series starts on television
Soviet spy ring caught in London
Jaguar launch their E-Type sports car
Beatles perform at the Cavern in Liverpool
Tottenham Hotspur win the double.
Acker Bilk's *Stranger on the Shore* becomes a major hit.
The birth control pill becomes available.

CHAPTER 12

The Big Fight – Charnley v Boggis

With the dawning of a new year, Dave Charnley could not have been in a better position. On the boxing front he was universally recognised as the number one challenger for the world championship, and many felt that he was now the new 'champion in waiting'. He still held the European, British and Empire titles, and Britain's leading promoters were falling over themselves to have him on their fight programmes. He was a wealthy young man, who had branched out into the business world, with a hairdressers shop already up and running and another planned for nearby Gravesend. These were ventures designed to safeguard his financial future once his boxing career came to a close.

Dave was still only 26 years old and probably just approaching his physical prime in terms of professional boxing, at least as far as the lighter weight categories were concerned. The boxing press were rightly claiming he was the biggest draw in British boxing, he was well known throughout the country thanks to appearing regularly on television, and was popular in Kent where both Dave and Ruth were often featured opening fetes and attending fund raising events. Although still painfully quiet and modest, it has to be acknowledged that he was no longer the one dimensional sportsman whose every waking hour was devoted to maintaining a super level of fitness. It was perhaps around this time in Dave's boxing life that earnings became equally, or maybe, more important than titles and the glory that came with them. This turnaround was probably as a result of his second loss to Joe Brown.

Dave's first fight of the year was scheduled for 25 January in Liverpool on a Mickey Duff promotion. Italian promoter Vittorio Strumolo was still determined to push ahead with a European title defence for Dave against Giordano Campari, a fight for which he had won the purse bids. However, the British Boxing Board were supporting Arthur Boggis's contention that this bid was invalid because the European bidding process had been concluded before Dave fought Hughes. As the Hughes fight did include a European defence Boggis argued that there should have been no bidding allowed until the outcome of that fight had been decided. With this in mind Boggis flew to Italy to meet Strumolo in early January in an effort to have the matter resolved.

As the fight approached, Duff had still not secured a suitable opponent. Nevertheless that Dave pressed ahead with his preparations, sparring many rounds with Fulham based Scot, Sammy McSpadden and Bermondsey welterweight Billy Tarrant. McSpadden's manager, Danny Mahoney, watched these sessions and remarked that he was continually telling the young Sammy to keep his left glove up to guard his chin. Mc Spadden learned that lesson the hard way being caught constantly with vicious right hooks. In the middle of these preparations Dave still found time to formally open the new Memphis Hall gym at Edge Hill owned by boxing manager, Bill MacDonald.

About ten days before the fight Dave learned that sitting in the opposite stool at Liverpool would be Jose Stable. There was nothing particularly worrying about the 21 year old Cuban although a year previously he had outpointed former world title challenger, Kenny Lane. Of 21 fights, Stable had won 19, losing only once. On paper it looked the ideal fight to start off the year.

A few days before the fight however, with Stable already in the country, and live television coverage agreed, Dave developed the flu. Boxers do get ill and with boxing not being a team game, there is little chance of bringing in a replacement at short notice to fill a top of the bill slot. Later Dave would admit he felt obliged to Duff and did not want to let him down. Duff also conceded that if the fight fell through it would be a financial disaster for him. Boggis and Dave discussed the problem and eventually in light of the financial considerations, Dave agreed to carry on. A delighted Duff offered Dave a bonus for going through with the fight. In any event the fight was simply postponed for five days to allow Dave to recover. The national boxing press on the day of the fight either virtually ignored the medical circumstances leading to the original delay or simply suggested that Dave was now fully recovered. They also played down the threat posed by Stable.

On 30 January a very healthy crowd of 3,500 turned up at Liverpool Stadium along with thousands watching live on television. What they saw was an extremely mellow performance from the man known as the Dartford Destroyer, who was clearly very much under the weather. Dave looked weak and unfit and seemed to be fighting in slow motion. Stable of course was fighting at the top of his game and this led to a close contest. At the final bell referee Lew Smith raised the Charnley arm to a chorus of booing from the Liverpool fans who had come along to see British boxing's star attraction. Many of the fans, and certainly Stable and his manager, felt he was robbed. However none of the ringside press saw it that way and all agreed Dave had deservedly won a very close decision. They were not impressed though and it is fair to say they slated him. Dave went back to his dressing room and lay down face first on the treatment table, the position he was still in when the press were admitted some ten minutes later. Dave told the reporters that he had fought too soon after his illness and had to conserve his strength throughout the fight. Boggis then went to settle up with Duff and returned soon after with the purse money but without the promised bonus. On Dave's insistence Boggis went back to Duff. When he returned he handed Dave a brown paper parcel. On opening it up Dave found it contained a dinner-service! Many decades later Duff was discussing this fight in the company of Dave's older brother William. William reminded Duff of the *dinner-service* bonus and he remarked that 'you can't get cash at wholesale prices!'

In the early hours of the following morning, while still in their Liverpool hotel, Ruth woke to find Dave sick and shivering in bed. She immediately contacted the hotel reception and asked for a doctor to be called. At the same time Ruth contacted reporter Reg Gutteridge who was in a nearby room and they both comforted Dave until Dr Kevin Ryan arrived. Arthur Boggis who was at the railway station awaiting a train to London was called back. The doctor thought it was a recurrence of the flu, while Boggis told Gutteridge that this was the third time

Dave had had this reaction after a fight and it was simply a nervous response! Ruth had been very angry about the fight taking place and was determined he should have a lengthy rest. Dave told Gutteridge that he had gone through with the fight as a favour because he didn't like letting anyone down but insisted that it would never happen again. From these comments it is easy to see the early shoots of a breakdown in the relationship between Dave and Boggis.

This did not stop Dave and Boggis travelling to Italy to attend the Italian Sports Writers awards ceremony in February. It was no coincidence that they both sat alongside Vittorio Strumolo and prospective challenger for the European title, Giordano Campari. Dave was present so he could receive the sports writers prize for being the European boxer of the year for 1961. Dave still has the tall green onyx trophy he received that night.

It was no surprise to learn that a few weeks following their return from Italy it was announced that the long delayed fight with Campari would go ahead on 18 May in Milan. What was surprising is the fact that at the beginning of May, it was also announced that Dave would be fighting on Solomons traditional Eve of the Derby show on 5 June just eighteen days after his proposed joust with Campari! Four top notch opponents had been proposed by Solomons – Flash Elorde, Carlos Hernandez, Paolo Rosi and Doug Vaillant.

On 21 April, in Las Vegas, 'Old Bones' Joe Brown finally lost his world crown to Carlos Ortiz by a clear and undisputed points decision. Soon after, and was it purely a coincidence, Dave's fight with Campari was called off and re-arranged for

5 July. Reports suggested that Dave had torn a calf muscle. Dave can't recall now the details of why this fight was cancelled, but the bad experience he had in Liverpool must have been playing on his mind. This had been a confusing few months for Dave following his troubled fight with Stable, plus the on-off nature of his European title defence and the possibility of a third crack at the world title due to promoter Jack Solomon's close relationship with champion Ortiz's manager, Bill Daly. His training plans were obviously disrupted and a damaged calf muscle would not have been an unusual outcome for a professional sportsman who was continuously stopping and starting in the build up to a contest.

With only a couple of weeks remaining until the Eve of the Derby show, Dave eventually learned that his opponent was to be Doug Vaillant. The Cuban born fighter was 24 years old and ranked number three in the world. He'd had 36 fights, winning 28 and losing just 4. He had beaten Len Matthews in 1960, lost on points to the new world champion, Carlos Ortiz, a year later, and in 1962 had beaten Fernand Nollet decisively on points. Once again Dave was fighting a ranked fighter but he had fought these contests before, and with his bout of flu long gone and the injured leg muscle now healed, his fans were confident that the return to the capital after an eight months exile would see another Charnley victory. The newspaper reporters, while supporting this view, had seen the Cuban in training and were impressed. They thought the fight would be close.

On 5 June Dave and his army of loyal fans made their way to Wembley in keen anticipation. Promoter Jack Solomons said in the programme for the fight that as Charnley was ranked number two and Vaillant one position below, if Dave should win he would go on to fight the champion, Carlos Ortiz in September, providing the rumours that Joe Brown would never box again were true. In any event both the fans and the media enjoyed a first class contest but they did not get the result most hoped for. Dave boxed as well as he had ever done in the first few rounds and he looked fit and appeared ready to take over. However, from around the 5th round the fight began to veer away from Dave. Vaillant had identified a weakness in Dave and that was an apparent inability to avoid right hand counters. The Cubans left jab was finding its way home and the right hands were scoring regularly. Vaillant began now to push forward and was no longer content to move around the ring. Dave seemed to be heavy legged and his opponent took over the fight. In the 8th session, with most thinking the fight was even, Vaillant landed with two rights to the head and a left to the body and a hurt Charnley staggered towards the Cuban, holding on for his life. When referee Eugene Henderson broke them up Dave was bleeding badly from the nose and looked troubled. In the next round Vaillant let go with a right and after it landed Dave plunged forward head first onto the canvas. He took the full nine count before getting to his feet. In the last round, Dave, sensing the fight was slipping away, came forward in attack, which was to prove his undoing. Vaillant took his time and sent in a crushing right hook to the solar plexus and Dave dropped onto all fours. Another count of nine followed before he managed to get up. Everyone knew Dave had lost and referee Henderson had no hesitation in raising Vaillant's arm.

The following day several boxing correspondents, most

notably Harry Carpenter, were reporting an important summit at Dave's home with Arthur Boggis. Ostensibly this was to discuss whether or not Dave would go ahead with his European title defence on 5 July in Milan. On reading between the lines it is clear that Boggis had been opening up to reporters about what he thought was going on behind the scenes. For instance Boggis had told Carpenter and Sydney Hulls that the Milan fight would net Dave £6,500 but he added the barbed comment that this would be a lot more than he would earn in a year as a hairdresser. We can take it from this that Boggis was not happy and that he felt this new enterprise was distracting Dave from his boxing career. Two interesting points emerge from this. Firstly, using the proposed Campari fight as an example, although the purse was £6,500, Boggis's managerial cut would have been 25%, or £1,600. Secondly, and perhaps more significant, Dave said nothing. None of the boxing press people published anything in relation to Dave's opinions, not even Reg Gutteridge with whom he was close. Regardless of the apparent dissent among the camp the Campari fight fell through and never did take place.

What did transpire was an unexpected defence of Dave's Empire title. Although he did defend it against Hughes this had been the only occasion since he beat Willie Toweel more than three years previously. The fight, scheduled for 4 August in Jamaica, would turn out to be more of an event than an actual boxing match. It was to be held on Jamaican Independence Day and would also be fought shortly after the official opening ceremony of the National Stadium in Kingston, performed by Princess Margaret, the Queen's sister. His challenger was local fighter Bunny Grant who from the outset seemed to be cast in the role of an *extra* for a film. George Leslie Grant, to give Bunny his Sunday name, was 21 years old and had 30 fights winning 25 and losing only 3. However he had never fought anywhere else other than Jamaica and Panama and the only recognisable name on his record was future *great* Jose Napoles. This had got to be considered a lucrative but relatively safe title defence for Dave.

Dave, accompanied by Ruth, flew on a Boeing 707 flight from London Airport to Kingston and were accommodated in the beautiful Courtleigh Manor complex in Montego Bay. It was clearly going to be a huge occasion for the Jamaican people and the two major newspapers on the island covered Dave's preparations on a daily basis. Three days before the fight Dave rounded off his sparring by boxing six rounds with local lads, Rick McMaster and Wesley Hinds, in front of the media. On the same day the media circus visited Grant's training camp and saw him sparring with deceptively named, Kid Banga. However all was not well with Dave. He had picked up a severe stomach bug which meant that for several days he was spending hours lying in bed curled up suffering from painful cramps. With the heat and the dehydration, Dave approached Boggis and told him he couldn't go ahead with the fight. Boggis was in a flap and visited the Jamaican boxing officials. When he came back he told Dave that they were going to withhold all the money, would not pay his hotel bill, nor would they pay the cost of his return flight to London. Dave felt totally drained and weak and felt he couldn't fight. Boggis told him that the only way out was for him to go ahead with the fight and to 'lie down' in the first round!

On the morning of the fight Dave failed to make the weight. He was half a pound over but managed to lose this reasonably quickly. During the build up to the fight there was even extensive coverage on how the ring would be built between Princess Margaret's opening ceremony and the 10.30pm start time for the fight.

Dave started the contest well enough and over the first two rounds there were no indications of the major upset which would unfold. By the halfway stage it was becoming clear that Grant was in control. In the 8th a crunching left from Grant opened a cut over Dave's right eye. In the same round Dave received another cut on the forehead as both boxers tumbled to the ground in an untidy tangle. In the 10th and 12th rounds Dave had to hang on as the young and inexperienced Jamaican landed with solid right hands. Dave was suffering heavy punishment to head and body as the fight drew to a close. Grant's inexperience showed briefly in the 15th round. He had clearly shot his bolt and had very little left allowing Dave to drive forward in a desperate attempt to turn things his way.

When the scorecards were read out at the end of the fight, embarrassingly for Dave, two judges hadn't given him a round! Dave looked a totally dejected fighter. He had cuts over both eyes, a cut on his forehead and his face was puffed and swollen. It can only be imagined how physically drained he must have been. The fact they he lasted the fifteen rounds is testament to his fighting heart.

The following day Dave and Ruth checked out of their hotel without speaking to Boggis and left the island. The manager never even knew they had gone. When Dave got back to Britain he at last broke his silence to Sydney Hulls of the Daily Express. Hulls was told that Dave had sacked Boggis and wanted to manage himself from now on. Dave raged that he would never have Boggis back in his corner and he didn't want anything to do with him again. It was reported that the row started three days before the Grant fight. Dave had been feeling ill and weak from a combination of a stomach upset and the tremendous heat. Dave had asked Boggis to call the fight off, and according to Dave, Boggis had said things to him which would never be forgiven. Of course this has all been confirmed years later but we now know what Boggis had actually said. Dave went on to tell Hulls that after the Stable fight in January, Boggis couldn't have cared less and had left for the London train knowing he was ill. Moreover, Boggis had not put in an appearance at training for six weeks leading up to the aborted Campari fight in May. When he pulled a leg muscle he had to search for Boggis to let him know that the fight would have to be cancelled. There had apparently been further problems with the Campari fight, and Dave had to deal with them himself as Boggis was on holiday. Boggis, in response, told Hulls that he was fed up with Charnley and that when he got home from Jamaica he would advise Dave to quit.

The fallout wasn't resolved and moved to the next stage. In late October, at the Boxing Board's premises, the Southern Area Council met to try to reach a solution to the impasse. Dave sat in one room and Boggis was in another with the only communication between them being through their respective lawyers. Dave attended the meeting with Ruth, his lawyer and a friend, ex-boxer and now a publican, Tommy Gibbons, while

Boggis had hired a barrister. Nothing was settled at that time although the Council representative declared that progress had been made. In actual fact Dave was advised that legally their contract was binding for another two years. He would have to continue working with Boggis or give up fighting. Dave chose to fight on but the nature of their relationship changed for ever. Boggis no longer had any say in training arrangements or the employment of sparring partners. Dave paid no heed to anything Boggis said in relation to an upcoming fight. Moreover Dave made sure he knew in great detail about the background to all future contests before he signed any contract.

There is an inference from what Boggis's was saying to the press that Dave may not have been as committed to his boxing career as he once had and that Boggis had become frustrated by this. Dave maintains that, even at this late stage in his career, he still trained every day, as if there was no tomorrow, and brothers Joe and William can confirm that. What caused the rift was more to do with a change in the manager / boxer relationship. From Dave's earliest days as a professional in late 1954, he had simply trained, sparred and fought whenever he had been told by his manager. He never questioned anything Boggis did, or suggested. But as he got older, and perhaps more aware, he began to ask questions of Boggis regarding which fights were being arranged, what the contracts stipulated and why some fights never took place. Boggis really resented this, and we have to ask ourselves why? Did he have something to hide or did he simply feel that Dave, unjustifiably, didn't trust him?

Realising that legally he was stuck with Boggis, Dave got back down to the business of fighting. He was contracted to fight at the Royal Albert Hall on a bill put together by new promoter, Mike Barrett. Barrett owned a wharf finger on the Thames and used his wealth to secure a contract to promote at the famous London venue. Although he had promoted at small halls previously this was his first step into the big time. For this fight Dave was trained by the overseer of the Thomas à Beckett, Danny Holland.

In opposition on 11 December was a man from Trenton, New Jersey, JD Ellis. But let's give him his proper title because it might raise a few eyebrows – James Dartford Ellis! Ellis was 23 years old when he met Dave, and from 44 fights had won 25. Over the previous two years he had lost by knockouts to Doug Vaillant and Lennie Matthews, and on points to Duillio Loi and Giordano Campari. However since he arrived in Britain in October he had taken less than three rounds to knock out decent British boxers, Dave Coventry and Brian Jones.

On the afternoon of the fight, following the weigh in, Dave and his camp retired to a Soho restaurant as was usually the case. Completely by surprise, they were joined by Arthur Boggis, who Dave had not spoken to for some months. There was a shaking of hands and a partial truce but Boggis was not allowed in Dave's corner for the fight. Afterwards Dave, diplomatically, told reporters that it would not have been sensible having Boggis in the corner as he had not seen him train in preparation for the contest.

Fortunately Dave's light shone brightly again for this fight, as he totally outclassed the American. Ellis strode out at the start and landed three jabs in succession. Briefly the fans thought Dave's recent poor form was going to continue but he started winging those right hands into Ellis and by the end of the 1st the visitor was cowering near the ropes and lost his way back to his own corner when the bell rang. Ellis got on his bike in the 2nd so much so that in his haste to avoid the advancing Charnley he tripped over one of the ring ropes and fell to the canvas, with referee Tommy Little counting to four over him. For the remainder of the fight Ellis took a one sided pasting from a re-born Charnley and after two minutes of the 6th round Tommy Little had seen enough and stopped the fight.

Afterwards in his dressing room, Dave seemed more confident and told the press he felt he was coasting until the 4th round, at which point he realised he could finish the fight inside the distance. He then stepped up a gear causing the early intervention two rounds later. As a footnote, there was an almost ceremonial shaking of hands for the press between Dave and Boggis.

1962 had been a poor year for Dave, certainly the worst he had experienced since turning professional. There had been injuries and illness which could perhaps have explained the under par performances against Stable and Grant, both of whom should not have troubled a top form Charnley. Vaillant had been a different matter all together – he was a world class operator, of that there is no doubt. How much were the *out of hours* issues with Boggis effecting Dave's preparations? Did Dave have other things on his mind in relation to his business? Was his heart still in the 'fight game'?

Historical Note – 1962
Z-Cars and Steptoe and Son first shown on television
James Hanratty hanged for A6 murder

The new Ford Cortina hits the road
Spurs beat Burnley in FA Cup final
Telstar satellite transmits programmes across the Atlantic
Bonnington and Clough become first Britons to conquer the North Face of the Eiger
Sunday Times print their first colour supplement.

CHAPTER 13

Revenge at Last and the Lonsdale Belt

While Dave may have been happy now that Boggis had been removed from the day-to-day involvement in his boxing career things must have felt a bit unsettling. For over eight years, since Dave was only 19 years old, Boggis had been a permanent fixture both at training and in his corner when fighting. They had been through a lot together. From the disputed decision after the second fight with Gracia, the hand injury which prevented him being at his best against Ortiz, and all the disappointment resulting from Tommy Little's decision following his second attempt at the world title. However there was a pattern of behaviour by Boggis which showed he didn't really have Dave's best interests at heart.

The first example of this was his attitude to sparring partner, Bob Paget, when Bob advised Boggis that Dave wasn't strong enough to go ahead with the fight with Willie Lloyd in Cardiff. He then encouraged Dave to fight Stable in Liverpool while clearly suffering from the effects of the flu, and then there was the disgraceful circumstances surrounding the loss of Dave's Empire title in Jamaica. Ironically, officials within the Boxing Board were passing *knowing looks* to one another whenever Dave called fights off, so much so that we recall the time their Secretary visited Dave at home with promoter Stan Baker to confirm he was actually ill. How often were fights called off due to behind the scene deals Boggis was making outwith Dave's knowledge? Arthur Boggis is no longer around to defend himself and maybe he would have been able to strongly refute these suggestions. Indeed at least one other boxer whom he managed did not have a bad word to say about the man and Dave himself never had any arguments with him of a financial nature.

As had become customary in previous years, Dave would find 1963 kicking off with a January bout against yet another American, Jethro Cason, known as Jetro. Cason, from Philadelphia, to be frank, was not in Dave's league. He'd had 23 fights winning 17 and losing 5. The only common opponent was JD Ellis, whom Cason had beaten twice on points.

The press were already speculating that following this fight Dave would then take on Maurice Cullen for the British title, with a victory securing him the coveted Lonsdale Belt for keeps. Thereafter he would at long last defend his European title against Giordano Campari before making a third attempt at the world crown against Carlos Ortiz.

On 15 January on a Jack Solomons promoted show at the Royal Albert Hall Dave faced the 25 year old American with the Thomas à Beckett duo, Danny Holland and Tommy Gibbons, in his corner. Cason had rashly predicted a 7th round knockout victory and this gave Dave an added incentive. Right from the start Dave opened up with solid rights to the head followed swiftly with lefts to the midriff. Only in the 4th did Cason look any threat to Charnley when he fired over two hard right crosses which seemed to worry the British champion. This spurred Dave on and he produced a performance which showed he was coming back to his best. He saved his best for the 7th when he picked his punches and was clearly hurting the visitor. Dave gave a little nod of satisfaction towards Cason when the round drew to a close as if to say 'That'll teach you!'. In the next round Charnley doubled Cason over with a left hook to the body and between rounds referee Jack Hart asked the Philadelphian if he wanted to continue. Dave kept up the steady bombardment until the end of the 10th winning a convincing victory.

Within half an hour of the fight ending Boggis was seen outside the Charnley dressing room in deep conversation with Boxing Board president, Onslow Fane, who doubled up as president of the European Boxing Union. The EBU had a meeting scheduled for 1 February and Onslow Fane, anticipating an attempt to strip Dave of his European title due to his failure to meet Giordano Campari, was urging Boggis to get a date and venue agreed beforehand. Boggis told the press that he would be contacting Campari's manager Steve Klaus and promoter Strumolo who had won the right to stage the fight. Boggis was still dissatisfied with the money on offer and was hoping to get the Italian to come to Britain. At the same time it was clear that Boggis had several irons in the fire. He was also trying to delay a British title fight with Maurice Cullen, using the possibility of this contest also including the European title, should Dave beat Campari. Not satisfied in dealing with the Italians and Cullen's people, Boggis was also hinting about a third option but was keeping the details of this close to his chest.

Once again the animosity between Dave and Boggis was evident the night after the Cason fight. Dave attended the Sports Writers annual dinner at the Waldorf Hotel with Boggis being a noticeable absence at the *boxing* table which included

Harry Gibbs, Bert McCarthy, Tim Riley from the Boxing News, Teddy Waltham and Reg Gutteridge.

Boggis's secret plans came to fruition in early February, and they provided a bombshell. Dave would be matched with old foe, Joe Brown, for a third time, although, of course he was no longer the world champion. On the same day the EBU took Dave's European crown off him and declared the title vacant. This proved to have been a major miscalculation by Boggis. He obviously hoped that he had persuaded Strumolo and Klaus to once again accept a delay to the Campari fight, but this plan had backfired with financial consequences for Dave, himself, and ultimately British promoters. There was no doubt that the Brown fight would prove lucrative but it seems like a case of 'short term gain, for long term loss'. The loss of the European title without a punch being thrown still rankles with Dave to this day. Nevertheless, the Italians and the EBU cannot be blamed, after all, the purse bids had been won fifteen months previously and the title had lain dormant since the defence against Hughes.

The world rankings were produced before the Brown fight and they showed just how much Dave's stock had dropped over the previous year. Champion was Carlos Ortiz and the challengers were Kenny Lane, Paul Armstead, Carlos Hernandez, Bunny Grant, Doug Vaillant, Eddie Perkins, Louis Molina, Joe Brown, Dave Charnley and Alfredo Urbina.

The *revenge* fight with Brown was scheduled for Belle Vue in Manchester on 25 February with Harry Levene promoting. Since Dave's battle with Brown for the world title almost two years previously, 'Old Bones' had fought four times. He had retained his title against Bert Somodio before losing to Ortiz. He had then lost to Louis Molina on points before stopping Tony Noriega in the 6th round in his last fight and of course he was still rated one position above Dave.

Harry Levene made it known that he had been in contact with Ortiz's manager Bill Daly and claimed he had a verbal agreement to stage a world title fight between the champion and whoever won the Brown versus Charnley contest. Levene even put it about that such a fight may take place in May or June, outdoors, at either Old Trafford or Maine Road, Manchester. Of course Levene and the British boxing press both hoped that Ortiz would be facing Charnley.

Both Brown and Dave had entered the business world since their last fight and in addition Brown claimed to have attained a four handicap at golf, demonstrating perhaps that his boxing career may have been winding down. He was 37 years of age and nobody would have criticised him if had hung up the gloves. However, this turned out to be well wide of the mark. After this fight with Dave, Brown fought a further 43 times finally quitting the ring for good in August 1970. Of those extra fights, 'Old Bones' was stopped only four times, and his ageing body managed to bring him 18 victories. At the weigh-in Brown still arrived three quarters of a pound inside the lightweight limit with Dave two pounds heavier so it can be assumed that Brown saw this fight as a possible route back to challenging for his old title.

Although there were no titles at stake and the fight had been moved out of London to Manchester, a very large crowd of 5,600 turned up. They were looking forward to seeing a former world champion, but also to pass judgement on Dave's future prospects. Was the Dartford Destroyer about to be put into dry dock for de-commissioning, or was he back into world title contention? There can be little doubt that a third defeat from Brown would have left him with very few options.

Scotsman Benny King, currently a well respected *cut man*, remembers being invited to spar with Brown in the build up to the fight. Brown's management team had been looking to engage southpaws, but had so far been unsuccessful. They were using a local welterweight, Charlie Grice, for his strength, but concluded they needed somebody around Dave's height for accuracy work. King's manager Stan Skinkiss, a former Charnley victim, supplied his man. Benny sparred with Brown for three days a week during the fortnight prior to the fight at Albert Marchant's gym in Salford. He says that Brown was very tall at the weight and also very strong. There was no doubt in Benny's mind that Brown had came to Britain to win.

Unfortunately, after all the work he had put in to arrange the bill, promoter Harry Levene took ill with a virus and was unable to see the fruits of his labour. As it turned out he missed a vintage performance from Dave which showed he was back to his brilliant best. Dave's display delighted the large crowd, and they quickly got into full swing in the 1st round when Dave threw himself across the ring at Brown throwing hooks and uppercuts in a determined effort to take control. Brown tried in vain to keep Charnley off but he just couldn't hold back the storm. In the 2nd Brown was warned by referee Frank Wilson to keep his punches up as he attempted to get into the fight and he did have some success with his rights. In the next round Brown seemed to be gaining the upper hand and he scored frequently with left jabs.

In the 4th Dave came out even more aggressively and ignoring Brown's jabs he bore in and hooked away to Brown's midriff. Two right hooks from Charnley troubled Brown and ringsiders could sense that the older fighter was wilting. In the following round Dave kept up the pressure and it was clear the old champion was suffering. Again referee Wilson had to warn Brown for illegal use of the head, but Dave just kept going, picking off his opponent with a right followed by a couple of lefts which almost forced Brown's gumshield out. Very early in the 6th Dave stiffened Brown with a powerful right that travelled only a few inches and the old timer was hanging on grimly. Charnley sensed the trouble Brown was in and went for the kill. A flurry of body shots drove Brown across the ring before a right to the heart and a left to chin, finally, after two fights and six and a half rounds, put 'Old Bones' on the deck. Joe managed bravely to get to his knees at six but he couldn't make it up before the referee counted him out. It was a glorious victory for the British champion and it proved to everyone he was back in business although there was a lot of sympathy for Brown. Nobody likes to see a great old champion being chopped down so convincingly but that's the way of boxing at the top. Afterwards Brown's camp tried to claim that he had been *thumbed* in the eye but this was only an excuse – he had been hit with a thumb, four fingers and a fistful of knuckles!

It was now full steam ahead towards the 22 April date, once again at Belle Vue, to defend his British crown against the mandatory challenger, Maurice Cullen. A victory in this fight would secure ownership for Dave of the coveted Lonsdale Belt, the rule being that three wins in championship contests meant the belt belonged to the victor for all time. However, not for the first time, Dave was struck down with the flu and the contest was postponed until 20 May. In the meantime the world rankings had been produced and Dave had moved up to number six in the list of challengers thanks to his win over Brown.

Maurice Cullen was a tough coal miner from Shotton in County Durham and had earned the right to fight Dave thanks to winning a series of eliminating contests culminating in a victory over Johnny Cooke. The 25 year old had engaged in 28 fights, winning 24 and losing only 2. He had beaten Dave's old bogey fighter, Guy Gracia, but significantly he had lost to former sparring partner, Sammy McSpadden. In preparation for this fight the North East man had taken himself down to Wales where he sparred with welterweight, Brian Curvis.

During the week leading up to the fight Harry Levene's matchmaker, Mickey Duff, told the press he had spoken to Ortiz's manager, Bill Daly, via a transatlantic telephone call to Englewood, New Jersey. He had arranged a fight between the winner of the Cullen and Charnley bout, and Ortiz, the fight being scheduled for either 10 September or 12 November in London.

On the night of the fight another huge crowd turned up in Manchester, swelled by busloads of Cullen fans, who cheered their man to the rafters. Dave came out in the 1st and took the centre of the ring, clearly intent on controlling the pace of the fight against the light footed Northerner. In the build up to the fight the boxing press had noted that Cullen did not possess a destructive punch and almost always relied on his speed and left jab to carry his fights. The 2nd was also a quiet round with only one meaningful punch landing, a right from the champion, causing a red mark near Cullen's eye. In the next round a left to the chin made Cullen stagger, and as he grabbed Dave's waist, he was swung to the floor bringing boos from the North East support. In the 4th Dave started to land with body shots and Cullen was feeling them. The pace dropped in the 7th as Cullen began to tire and this allowed Charnley to pick his punches and win the round comfortably. By the 10th round Cullen's left eye was closing rapidly and during the following session a left hook to the body put him down for a brief count. In the 12th he seemed to be nearing the end, however a rousing chorus of the *Blaydon Races* from the rear of the stands seemed to spur him on and he managed to paw with his jab and move away throughout the last three rounds to enable himself to last the distance. After fifteen tepid rounds referee Bill Jones lifted Charnley's arm and the belt was won outright. Boos rang out at this result puzzling ringside observers. It was clear that Dave had won convincingly in fact most of the press had Dave winning at least nine rounds. It is likely that the crowd had been expecting fireworks from Charnley and were disappointed when he fought conservatively. In the dressing room later Dave expressed the view that he knew that Cullen didn't possess a punch to trouble him and that he felt he would benefit from travelling the full distance. Cullen would go on to win the British title in future years only losing it subsequently to Ken Buchanan.

Two weeks after the fight Dave and Ruth were off once again for a month to their favourite destination, Juan Les Pains, in the

South of France. He went there in the knowledge that there were hopeful signs of a world title challenge to Ortiz in September at Wembley. With victories over Cason, Brown and Cullen it looked like his career was back on track and those who were beginning to think he was winding down seemed to be very much mistaken.

Once the holidays were out of the way Dave had two issues on his mind. Firstly he was busy planning the building of his new home in Darenth Road, Dartford and also he knew he would need to commence his training for the Ortiz fight. Not long after the training started Dave suffered a body blow. The newly formed World Boxing Association, which really had very little formal recognition in those days, stripped Ortiz of his title because of his refusal to defend it against Kenny Lane. In Britain this meant next to nothing because the WBA were unrecognised and considered to be simply a self-appointed body. However, Ortiz believed that he needed the WBA on his side, particularly in relation to future fights in America, so he opted to attend a special meeting of that organisation to plead his case. This meant that he had to break training camp for the fight with Dave, and believing that he couldn't afford the time off, the fight in London was postponed. Harry Levene decided to push back the Wembley date to 10 September and promised to find a top notch American boxer for Dave. It is difficult to imagine how a fighter might feel when faced with this type of situation. His schedule of training is worked out in advance, designed in such a way that it ensures that he is in peak condition at fight time. Sparring is organised so that more and more rounds are added each week as the contest approaches. The boxers weight is being monitored making sure that he is on schedule to reach the limit on the day of the fight. How do they cope when a fight is cancelled in the midst of these preparations?

Arthur Boggis was not letting the grass grow under his feet, and, quite rightly, was making moves to continue his managerial career into the future. Despite fierce competition, he signed up Fisher ABC amateur heavyweight, Roy Enifer, who at that time was considered the next 'Golden Boy'. Boggis, of course, was still heavily involved in negotiations with Harry Levene regarding Dave's next opponent and eventually Levene secured the services of Roberto Tito Marshall. Although the Charnley and Marshall fight was to be top billing it was becoming overshadowed by the visit of world heavyweight champion, Sonny Liston. Liston was in the midst of a tour of Britain and was scheduled to make an appearance at Wembley performing his famous skipping routine. Also causing greater interest, now that a world championship fight had been cancelled, was the heavyweight showdown between the original 'Golden Boy', Billy Walker, and his main rival at this time, Johnny Prescott.

Further bad luck fell on Dave some ten days before the fight when he injured his left hand in sparring. This was the same injury he had sustained before the fight with Carlos Ortiz in 1958 and the visible signs of this repeated damage can still be seen today. Boggis had no option but to advise Levene that his main contest was off and of course this again allowed the growing number of doubters to speculate that Dave's heart wasn't in it any more. A few weeks later as the hand was beginning to heal, and as if to add insult to injury, it was announced that Ortiz would be coming to London after all only

9

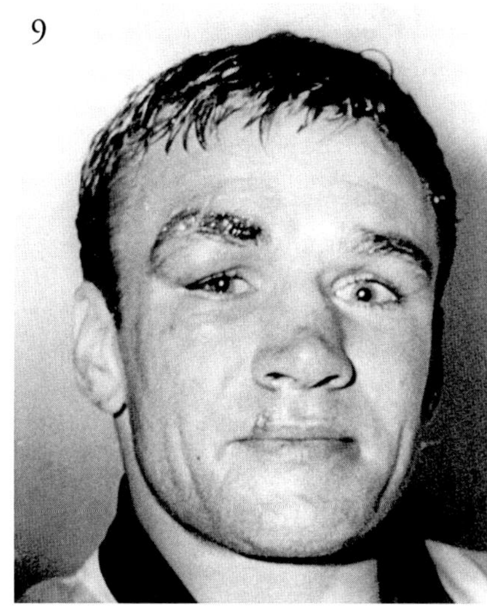

9: The cut eye which ended Dave's first world title challenge in Texas. *10:* The ever reliable, Ray Bartlett, wipes down Dave's sparring gloves.

10

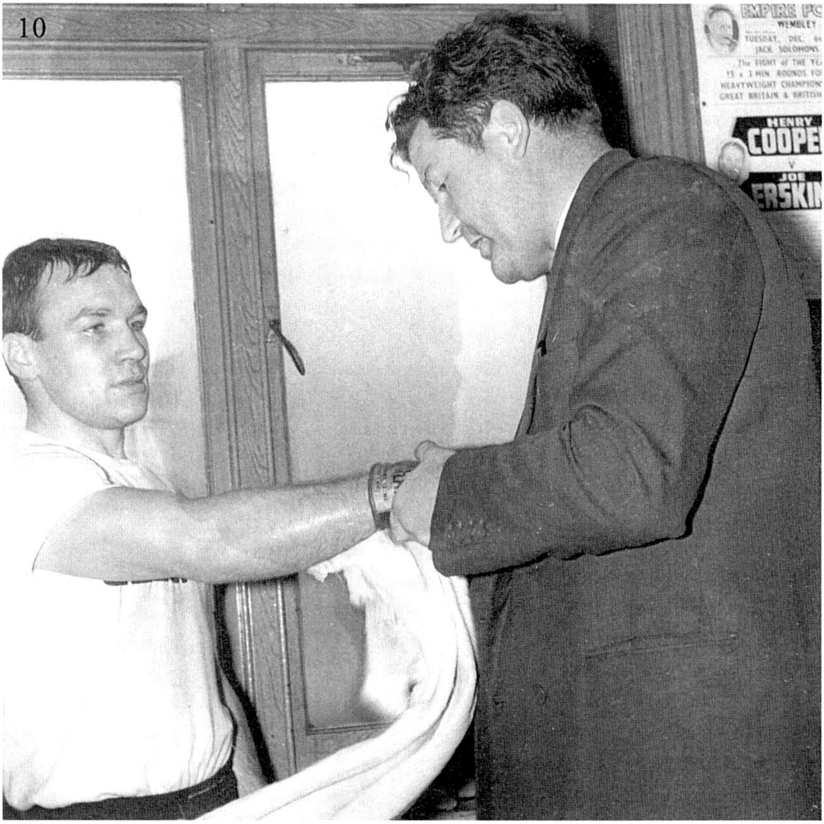

This page: 11: Dave and Joe Brown battling for the world title at Earls Court. *12:* 14 February 1962 in Italy. Shaking hands with Giordano Campari after Dave received the award as the outstanding European boxer of 1961. *Opposite page: 13:* Early 1970s and Dave seems to be doing very well!

12

13

14: A family gathering at Christmas. *15:* Brothers William and Joe, with Mickey Duff, at Dave's 60th birthday. *16:* Daughters Lisa (left) and Joanna (right) admire Dave's Lonsdale Belt.

this time he would be fighting a non-title fight with former Charnley victim, Maurice Cullen. Again, we can only speculate at how demoralising these set of circumstances must have been for Dave. He had just turned 28 years of age and realised that his chances of reaching the top were being reduced. Old injuries were taking longer to clear up and it was becoming easier to throw himself into his business interests when he felt depressed about his boxing career.

It is interesting to observe that on 22 October Ortiz beat Cullen on points over ten rounds, but whereas Dave had been criticised by some for not stopping the light hitting Durham miner, Ortiz seemed to have escaped that particular barb. Soon after this Levene announced that Dave and Terry Downes would be the star attractions at Belle Vue Manchester on 25 November. Tito Marshall was again chosen as Dave's opposition.

With Ortiz now having visited Britain on two previous occasions, coupled with the fact that he was a regular traveller beyond the confines of America, it is extremely likely that he could have been encouraged to come again with his title at stake. Levene, Solomons, Boggis and Dave all knew this, as did the press. Dave's upcoming fight with Marshall was not an eliminator as such but he needed to put on a show to keep himself in contention.

Marshall, from Panama, had engaged in 40 fights, winning 29 and losing 9. Over the previous two years he had won and lost to Bunny Grant. What should have been more ominous for Dave and his team was that Tito was almost six inches taller and in his last three fights had weighed 10st, 10st 7lb and 10st 4lb. This contest was contracted at 10st, and significantly Marshall had Whitey Bimstein in his corner. Whitey was a very famous New York trainer. He had been in Harry Greb's corner when he fought Gene Tunney in 1923. He was in James J Braddock's corner when he won the world heavyweight title from Max Baer in 1935. He took Rocky Graziano to the world middleweight crown in the 1940s and guided Ingemar Johannson when he took the heavyweight championship from Floyd Patterson. As Whitey would have said, 'I don't travel with bums!'.

Dave was going through his paces at the Thomas à Beckett under the guidance of Danny Holland and had advertised for sparring partners offering £5 per day for the privilege. Come fight time Dave was in peak condition.

At the weigh in on 25 November Marshall hit the bar at 10st but there were mutterings that he had just made it. Dave weighed in at 9st 12lb. Given the circumstances it is entirely feasible that come fight time there would probably be at least half a stone difference in the weights. Marshall certainly looked much bigger when they entered the ring. The fight was televised by BBC's Sportsview programme, being shown the following evening.

Dave started quickly and managed to land with right jabs and left hooks to the head in the opening rounds. Marshall, using his reach caught Dave regularly with left leads and surprisingly for one so tall he caught Dave to the body when on the inside. In the 3rd round both went toe to toe for about half a minute and when they broke Marshall kept his ground and refused to back off. The fight slowed in the 5th but when the crowd became restless Dave went on the offensive landing a right and left to the Panamanian's chin. In this round Bimstein had instructed Marshall to switch to the southpaw stance and in the next this plan backfired somewhat when Dave took control and punished Marshall around the body. The 7th swung back towards the tall opponent and he landed cleanly with jabs and right uppercuts. The 9th was a bit of a maul with a lot of wrestling requiring the intervention of referee Wally Thom. Dave as usual came out for the last round determined to give it his all knowing that the fight was close. However it was Marshall who dominated throwing flurries of punches which seemed to stagger Charnley. At the end Dave moved towards the referee but Wally Thom lifted the arm of Marshall. Many felt that the last round had won it for the visitor although there were arguments both ways.

Afterwards the view from Dave was that Marshall had simply been too big and was really a welterweight and he vowed never to fight out of his weight class again.

A strange year came to an end with Dave's star on the wane. He had clinched the Lonsdale Belt for life and exorcised the ghost of Joe Brown, but at the same time had lost out on another world title opportunity. The hopes of that fight coming to fruition seemed damaged by the loss to Marshall although there was a case to be made that Marshall was not really a lightweight. His finances were in good order and his dream home had been completed but in the year the Dartford Tunnel opened, was the Dartford Destroyer's career simultaneously coming to a close?

Historical Note – 1963
The year of the Great Train Robbery
The Hillman Imp launched
Beatles reach number one with *From Me to You*
Summer Holiday with Cliff Richard is a major cinema attraction
Douglas Home replaces Harold Macmillan as Prime Minister
President John F Kennedy assassinated

CHAPTER 14

The Curtain Comes Down

Dave entered 1964 as a 28 year old with a successful business, a new luxury home, a top of the range Jaguar car and celebrity status. Conversely he also had a damaged left hand, had just been defeated by an average Panamanian and was enduring an extremely strained relationship with a manager he didn't like, knowing there was a contract binding them together for a further year. So what was driving Dave on to continue his fistic career? It certainly was not because he needed the money. He also had no obligation to fulfil his contract with Boggis and being the shy and reserved individual he was, he was not seduced by a need to remain in the public eye. The reason was simple. He still retained a burning ambition to be the world champion, and while the possibility existed for a match with Carlos Ortiz, he just couldn't walk away.

It was around this time that the proliferation of world sanctioning bodies began. Ortiz had already suffered a bad experience with the embryonic WBA when he was initially stripped of his title, and now another organisation had emerged, this time the World Boxing Council, who also claimed the right to decide who the world champions and challengers should be. Of course, these self appointed bodies were not self funding! They generated income by charging promoters a *sanctioning fee* for the privilege of using their names to legitimise the title fights they put on. So in early 1964 Ortiz was ordered to firstly defend his crown against the WBC number one contender, followed shortly thereafter by another defence against the WBA top contender. This tied Ortiz up with mandatory fights until the summer at least and left Dave treading water.

On 15 February Ortiz successfully defended one of the titles with a 14th round technical knockout of Flash Elorde in the Philippines, with another scheduled defence set for 11 April against Kenny Lane in Puerto Rico. Dave was desperate for action, and Boggis was desperate to keep the eggs flowing from his *golden goose*. Promoter Jack Solomons was still a fan of Dave and knew he could pull in the crowds. Therefore he arranged for Dave to fight the British and Empire welterweight champion, Welshman Brian Curvis, at Wembley on 24 March. He had given both boxers the option of either fighting American opposition, or doubling their purse by fighting each other.

This was an inspired piece of business by Solomons, pitching the British champions at welterweight and lightweight against each other, a repeat of the 1958 scenario when Dave hammered Peter Waterman into retirement. And who promoted that fight, none other than Solomons himself!

While many felt that Waterman, although only 23 years old, was on the slide, the same could not be said of Curvis. The Cardiff man was 26 years old and had won 29 of 30 contests, and had avenged his solitary loss. He had won the Empire title in 1960 from George Barnes and added the British title that same year by beating Wally Swift. He had since made four successful defences of both crowns and was being lined up to challenge for the world championship. Although never out of condition, Curvis had stepped up a gear and was doing his preparatory training at St Ives in Huntingdonshire under the watchful eye of Anglo-Scot, Andy Smith. Smith would later gain fame as the trainer of Dave 'Boy' Green and Joe Bugner. Curvis's trainer as he approached the fight was, as usual, his brother Cliff.

The contracted weight for the fight was 10st 9lb, just over the welterweight limit, to ensure that Curvis's titles were not in any danger. However there were strong rumours that there was to be an unofficial weigh-in, held in private, on the insistence of the Charnley camp. The limit at that event was to be 10st 5lb, this being an attempt to prevent Curvis coming in at a much heavier poundage. The Boxing Board ignored this and as far as they were concerned there would only be one weigh-in.

In the programme notes for the fight Jack Solomons recorded that he had signed papers with Gil Clancy, manager of the world welterweight champion Emile Griffith, which guaranteed a fight with Curvis for the title, if he beat Charnley. On the other hand Solomons quickly glossed over any hopes he had in relation to a world championship tilt for Dave. Not encouraging omens if you happened to be in the Charnley camp.

Before the fighting even started at Wembley there was controversy. Jack Hart, who was supposed to referee another fight that night between Howard Winstone and Rafiu King, was removed from that contest after Winstone's manager, Eddie Thomas, protested. The Boxing Board upheld this, and moved Hart over to the Curvis and Charnley fight. This turned out to be a crucial decision as far as Dave was concerned.

In this battle of southpaws, the pre-fight betting overwhelmingly favoured the Welshman at 2-1 on. No one however would have taken those odds when the boxers came out for the last round. In the 1st round both fighters scored well and during a heated exchange the referee warned Curvis for coming in with his head. It was an excellent start to the fight and already the capacity crowd were on their feet. Curvis appeared to take the 2nd and although there was a lot of holding, Curvis scored cleanly with left handers. The fight swung back to Dave in the 3rd when a right and left hook caught Curvis and had him staggering. The Welshman clung on but Charnley threw him off and drove him to the ropes. Dave appeared to hit Curvis with his head and earned himself a rebuke. Curvis tried to regain the advantage in the 4th but as he threw a left cross, Dave ducked and came back with a thunderous right which again caused Curvis to wobble. Dave again seemed to take the 5th and Curvis ended the round with a cut over the right eye. The 6th and 7th were hard fought even affairs with Charnley storming forward and Curvis trying to outbox him. However Dave's fans were convinced that the 8th round should have decided matters in his favour. In this session, Dave came out and drove his man to the ropes where both boxers let go with hooks. Suddenly Charnley scored with a right to the body, a left to the jaw, and a final right to the chin which sent the welterweight champion to the deck. In the pandemonium which ensued, the actual count was lost, but Curvis did get to his feet on time. Dave was all over him and Curvis had to use all his experience to avoid going down again, and was lucky to hear the bell. The Welshman rallied strongly in the penultimate round as he realised Dave was exhausted after his previous efforts, so it was all down to the last. Once again Dave stormed forward and both boxers were standing toe to toe when the bell rang. Charnley approached referee Hart to have his arm raised and looked on in shock as the official walked over to Curvis and awarded him the fight. The boos rang out once again after yet another contentious decision against Charnley.

The following morning most reporters reckoned Charnley had won the fight but it was not unanimous by any stretch of the imagination. It had been close but the knockdown in the 8th seemed to have clinched it. Regardless of how people scored the fight, it had undoubtedly been a cracker and Jack Solomons knew this. With Ortiz and Griffith scheduled to fight in April, and Griffith defending his crown in June, world title fights in Britain for Dave or Curvis were unlikely to happen before September. Shrewd Jack needed to keep the *kettle boiling*, and what better way than matching the lightweight and welterweight champions again? This was a win-win situation for everyone. The fans and the press wanted it, the boxers and their managers wanted it, and Jolly Jack most certainly wanted it. The only potential loser out of all this could have been Brian Curvis because a defeat by the smaller Charnley could jeopardise his title chance against Griffith.

In the meantime however the pressure was mounting for Dave to once again defend his British title and the number one challenger was deemed to be Dave Coventry. Mike Barrett won the purse bids to promote the fight at the Royal Albert Hall on 28 April. However some six days before the contest an unnamed sparring partner broke Coventry's ribs and left him with a suspected punctured lung, necessitating a long spell in hospital. Once again Dave was left without an outlet for his stringent training regime. Fortunately for Dave, Jack Solomons wasn't slow off the mark, and he quickly set plans in motion for the Curvis and Charnley return fight.

With only nine days to go before the contest on 2 June, Solomons awoke on a Sunday morning to the news all promoters dread. Curvis had damaged his Achilles tendon and pulled out. With the Empire Pool at Wembley a virtual sell-out Solomons had to think fast in terms of a suitable replacement. Incredibly, when viewed from modern times, with only seven days to go, he secured the services of the number one lightweight contender, Kenny Lane, who had just lost a championship attempt to Ortiz two months previously. From Dave's perspective the whole nature of the fight changed overnight. No longer was he fighting someone whose style he knew well and who was half a stone heavier, but was taking on the slick fast moving Lane who would be attempting to remain at the top of the world rankings.

It could easily be argued that the 32 year old Michigan fighter was virtually the best boxer Dave had met until this time. *Virtually* only because he had just been beaten by Ortiz, but beyond that recent defeat his record was mightily impressive. He had engaged in 93 fights, winning 79 and losing only 12. He had beaten Johnny Gonsalves twice, Doug Vaillant, Len Matthews and Paul Armstead. He had also beaten Carlos Ortiz in 1958 although he was subsequently stopped in two rounds a year later on cuts for a version of the newly inaugurated light welterweight title. Like Dave, he was a southpaw.

At the weigh-in for a match, which Solomons was now billing as a final eliminator, both came in within the 9st 12lb limit. It later came out that in the morning Lane had found himself three pounds too heavy and apparently spent some time in a Turkish bath sweating off the excess.

There were many who ventured out to this Eve of the Derby show believing that this could be the end of the line for Dave. A defeat would leave him clinging on solely to his British title, and end any hopes he had of challenging Ortiz. With the Lonsdale Belt now in his possession, and being well off financially, what would be the point of continuing?

As it turned out, this quite possibly was Dave's finest hour in a boxing ring. The fight was universally considered to have been a classic with an aggressive boxer versus a skilful counter puncher. There was no feeling out factor in the 1st round as Dave jumped from his stool and launched into the attack with his right hand scoring freely. Dave was then forced onto the ropes by a barrage from Lane which also earned him a warning from Belfast referee Andy Smyth due to him using his forearm. The 2nd was a barnstormer with Dave landing cleanly with left hooks and Lane firing back with left uppercuts to the body. During this round Dave was cut over the right eye but this spurred him on and by the end of the round Lane had been hurt and holding on. A pattern was emerging, with Dave powering forward and Lane answering with accurate flurries, but it was clear that the Michigan man's punches were having no effect. This was Charnley who had seemingly turned back the clock and was back to his brilliant best.

During the middle rounds Dave eased off the throttle and

was picking his punches but when they landed they shook Lane down to his boots. Ringside reporters could sense that Lane knew he was falling behind and he would occasionally fire back with clusters of punches but they seemed to lack impact. By the 8th Lane was looking the worse for wear with a graze over his eye and bleeding from an injured mouth. At the start of the 9th, Dave went all out to finish matters and stormed into Lane with right and left hooks to the head, and although Lane tried to fight back, he was being overwhelmed. Charnley got him onto the ropes and let go with everything in his arsenal, this was the Dartford Destroyer in full flow. To most observers the bell to end the round saved Lane from being stopped. Both fighters rose for the last round to the cheering of the crowd who were roaring themselves hoarse. The boxers met in mid ring and staged a dramatic last round. Lane realising that his number one ranking was in danger tried to stand his ground and trade with Charnley but it was to no avail as once again he had to retreat under the onslaught. However, Lane almost snatched victory from the jaws of defeat. With a last throw of the dice the American threw everything he had into a left cross which landed flush on Dave's chin. Dave's arms dropped, his knees sagged, and he seemed on the point of going down. But miraculously he came to, and fired back just as the bell rang. The referee walked over to Charnley and declared him the victor to thunderous applause from the partisan crowd.

The next day Dave was talking to brother William and remarked that he was shocked when he read the newspapers and that they had highlighted the big punch Lane landed just before the end. He told William that he honestly felt it had not bothered him any more than other punches his opponent had landed during the fight.

Later American journalists would claim a *home town* decision, and Lane himself hinted at this. Rather unkindly he added that Dave would have no chance against Ortiz should they fight for the title. Even those British reporters who had begun to turn against the Dartford man had to concede that Dave won the fight convincingly, with most scoring the contest seven rounds to three. Jack Solomons immediately declared that providing Boggis reduced his purse demands for Dave, he would challenge again for the world title on 22 September.

Once again Dave went off on summer holidays totally convinced his next fight would be against Ortiz, exactly the same position he had been in the year before. A British title defence against Dave Coventry had been mooted in some quarters but in Dave's mind that was never really an option. Unfortunately Jack Solomons had nothing in writing for the proposed Ortiz fight and there were rival challengers for the right to fight him. Rafito Cedeno, manager of the Venezuelan champion, Carlos Hernandez, was offering Ortiz £20,000 plus expenses for him to travel to South America claiming that as his man had destroyed Tito Marshall and Doug Vaillant he was more deserving of the fight.

Towards the end of July there was further disquieting news for both Solomons and Charnley when American promoter Don Elbaum stated that he hoped to stage a world title bout between Ortiz and Johnny Bizarro in Pittsburgh towards the end of September. This fight didn't take place until two years later as it turned out! The first real indication Dave had that the

Ortiz fight had fallen through yet again was on 4 September when Solomons mentioned to the press that the fight was being put back to later in the year. This was only three weeks short of the scheduled date and Dave's preparations were at an advanced stage.

As expected, on 22 September, Brian Curvis did fight for the world welterweight title against Emile Griffith, losing on points over fifteen rounds. It is impossible now to ascertain with any certainty why it was Curvis and not Charnley who was fighting for a world title that night.

Even in 1964 the relatively new sanctioning bodies were causing consternation with their bizarre world rankings. The WBA for instance had listed Dave as their number six contender, with recent Charnley victims Kenny Lane and Paul Armstead rated number one and two respectively. At the same time the Boxing News still had Dave at number one on their entirely unofficial list.

With Dave having been out of action now for five months, a fight was arranged for 10 November against Valerio Nunez, an Argentinian who had been fighting recently in Italy. Once again, this scheduled Mike Barrett promotion had to be cancelled when Dave sprained his wrist and a doctor ordered a postponement. Barrett moved the promotion to 16 November when Henry Cooper headlined against Roger Rischer but he was far from finished with Dave and brought lawyers in to ensure that Dave would be forced to fight for him early in the new year.

Around this time older brother William remembers getting a phone call from Dave who sounded very excited. He had been told by Boggis that at long last the fight with Ortiz was on and that Dave had to meet his manager at the House of Commons. When he arrived there he met not only Boggis, but Emile Griffith, Griffith's manager Gil Clancy, Brian Curvis and Daily Mirror journalist Peter Wilson. It turned out that they had all been invited to lunch at the House of Commons by Arthur Lewis MP for West Ham. Griffith and the others sat through thirteen speeches by the Chairman of the Labour Party, Manny Shinwell, and afterwards the visibly emotional world welterweight champion told the waiting press that he couldn't believe he had actually sat in the 'mother of all parliaments'. When Dave was alone with Boggis he asked why he'd to pose for all the pictures with Griffith. It was only then that Boggis told him he'd be fighting the world welterweight champion on 1 December. When Dave started to protest Boggis told him he could either fight Ortiz for £5,000 or Griffith for £10,000. Needless to say, Dave, confident of beating both, took the latter option.

There could only have been one reason for Dave to take on Emile Griffith and that was money. There was talk that a victory in this non-title affair would qualify Dave for a return bout with the world welterweight championship at stake, but comments by Griffith's manager Gil Clancy, in later years, indicated that they had very little fears of that happening. Griffith was considered to be a *big* welterweight which meant that when not in full training for a contest he would weigh a lot heavier than the 10st 7lb limit requiring him to shed weight come fight time. In this type of circumstance, when a boxer needs to come down in weight for a weigh-in, his weight would usually increase significantly come the time of the fight.

In addition to this, at that time, Griffith had to be considered one of the world's best fighters. He was the reigning world welterweight champion and had won a lightly regarded version of a new world light middleweight crown. The Virgin Islander, now based in New York, had fought 48 times, winning 42 and losing 5. He won and then lost the welterweight title to Benny 'Kid' Paret in 1961. In a rematch Griffith had battered the defenceless Paret, who was being held up by the ropes, before the referee intervened. Tragically Paret never regained consciousness and died some time later in hospital. Griffith would win the world middleweight championship in 1966 and his last fight was against Alan Minter in 1977 at Monaco. Ominously for Dave, Griffith, when not fighting in title contests, usually weighed between 10st 9lb and 11st. With Dave always approaching contests in peak condition and carrying no excess weight it is almost certain that the most he could have weighed at fight time would have been 9st 13lb. The agreed weight on the contract was 10st 8lb to protect Griffith's welterweight title, but Boggis had stipulated that another unofficial weigh-in should take place one hour before the official version and at that time both fighters should come in under 10st 5lb. Both boxers done their training for the fight at the Thomas à Beckett with Dave starting off at 11am and Griffith taking over three and a half hours later, thereby ensuring that their paths didn't cross.

The fight at Wembley saw Dave attempt to storm forward and take the fight to the bigger man, but on this occasion, while brave, he was not big enough, strong enough or fast enough to cope with a superb champion at the very top of his game. From the first couple of rounds the crowd knew the inevitable outcome as they saw Charnley's punches bounce off Griffith while at the same time every time the New Yorker landed it seemed to shock Dave round down to his boots. In the 3rd round all hell broke loose when Griffith drove Dave on to the ropes and drove in a deadly hook to the body. The punch appeared to land below the border line and Dave slumped to the canvas. He rose at nine and grabbed on to Griffith for all he was worth. Glasgow referee Frank Wilson separated the boxers and gave Griffith a stern warning. Before the end of the round Griffith poured in five more punches and Dave was down again from a body shot but the bell rang before a count was administered.

Even at this early stage Dave's face was bashed up and he knew he was in a war. In the 5th Griffith was warned a second time for careless use of the head as the crowd began to voice their displeasure. At the end of the round Dave had another injury to contend with, this time a cut under his left eye. In the 6th Charnley landed with a good left hook which done nothing but goad Griffith into action and he peppered Dave with punches one of which caused the Dartford man to dab at his eye when he retreated towards Griffith's corner as the bell rang. In the 7th the one-sided beating continued and Dave was downed again but got up without taking a count.

The one way traffic carried on in the 8th as Griffith seemed to be getting stronger and faster with Dave's face now a mass of bumps and bruises. Between the 8th and 9th rounds, Clancy, in Griffith's corner, told his man to go out and finish it, and that's exactly what he did. After about a minute and a half there was an exchange of punches along the ropes and as Charnley reached a neutral corner post Griffith connected with a burst of punches, the last of which, a left hook, sent Dave down. The force of the punch and Dave's momentum caused him to land and somersault backwards landing on his knees. He looked over to his corner to signal he was all right but referee Wilson waved his arms and signalled that he had seen enough. Dave and his team accepted the decision but bizarrely it was Clancy who stormed into the ring and protested to the referee claiming that he had been over officious. Later Clancy told the press that he had instructed Griffith to only punch above the chest area for fear of him being disqualified. In the losers dressing room Dave was disappointed that he didn't see the fight out, and acknowledged he was well beaten. Typical of Dave, he said that he wanted to fight Griffith again.

Over the previous eighteen months Dave had seen two proposed world title challenges to Carlos Ortiz fall through. He had on three occasions been matched with heavier men, losing them all, with the one against Curvis being hotly disputed, and he had seen a re-match with Curvis, and a British defence against Dave Coventry all fall by the wayside. The frustration these events must have brought to Dave made him extremely despondent and following the heavy loss to Griffith he could see a third tilt at the world title disappearing over the horizon. When Jack Solomons announced a triple world title bill at an open air arena for June 1965 involving Dave against Ortiz, Winstone against Saldivar and a repeat of Curvis against Griffith, we can imagine a sense of cynicism from Dave and his camp.

On 1 January 1965 Mike Barrett advised the press that Dave would defend his British title against Dave Coventry at the Royal Albert Hall on 9 February. However within a fortnight of that news breaking, on 15 January, Dave made a public announcement that he was retiring from boxing. Not surprisingly Dave was overwhelmed by the flood of letters and telephone calls he received following this decision and he was moved to pen a personal letter of thanks which was published in the Boxing News on 29 January. At the time Dave made it clear, as did his manager, that the decision he had made was based purely on business reasons. He was becoming heavily involved with a new house building project and this coupled with his thriving hairdressing enterprise were proving to be distractions. Being someone who was totally committed to his fitness, and being in top condition for his fights, he would not accept anything less, and a decision had to be made one way or the other. He repeated this when interviewed by David Coleman for the BBC's Grandstand programme the following Saturday.

Although only 29 years old when he left the fight game, Dave never looked back. Occasionally when invited to the big fights up in London someone would ask if he would consider a comeback but this was never seriously contemplated. Another by-product of these nights was the fact that he couldn't stand watching the fights live. He enjoyed meeting old friends and was grateful for being remembered but there was something about the occasions which made him feel uncomfortable. Perhaps it was an inner sadness when he realised he wasn't part of the drama anymore? Usually when sports people look back on their careers there can be a great deal of nostalgia, but not with Dave. For those who have not been there this is difficult to understand, but he seems to have an ability to accept that this was a phase of his life which has gone and cannot be repeated, therefore there's no use dwelling on it!

When reviewing Dave's boxing career it is worth asking if it was as successful as it could have been. But *success* in these circumstances has two faces. The first concerns itself purely with sporting achievement, and the second with ££££ signs.

Dave retired as the undefeated British lightweight champion. He was the undefeated European champion when he was stripped for failing to defend the title against Campari. He held the British Empire, or Commonwealth, title before losing it in sad circumstances to an opponent he should have beaten with ease. He fought twice for the world crown against an extremely underrated and forgotten champion, losing controversially at the second attempt, this during an era in which boxing was probably the second most favourite sport in both Britain and America. This underlines just how much it would have meant to many people, not least of all Dave himself, if he had beaten Joe Brown.

In many ways, the latter end of the Charnley career, was overshadowed by the fights which didn't take place. Foremost amongst these was the oft times aborted fights with Carlos Ortiz. On three separate occasions these fights seemed to have been fixed. The first was before Ortiz beat Brown for the title. If Dave had beaten him then he would more than likely have got another chance at Brown. After Ortiz took over from Brown a further two opportunities presented themselves. Anything could have happened if these fights had gone ahead especially if they had been in London. When Dave did fight Ortiz in 1958, very few people other than the Charnley camp disputed the decision. Ortiz looked so much bigger than Dave and had strength to go with it. He was a superb fighter but it is also a fact that days before the fight Dave hurt his hands and had pain killing injections prior to entering the ring. What does it feel like when you throw a punch, and you have no sensation in your hand? Is it a distraction, are you able to fully concentrate on the tactics required to beat a world class performer? It is likely that Dave's left hand was probably broken and in later years he needed surgery to repair the damage brought through punching so powerfully. Over fifty years later the hand is still misshapen.

It must also be considered a mistake not to have defended his European title when contracted to do so. It is fairly likely that he would have beaten Campari and this could have allowed further defences in Britain and possibly encouraged Dave to continue his career beyond 1964. The benefit of this may have been that with the light-welterweight division starting to appear Dave would have been in a prime position to contest a challenge at the new 10st limit, giving him another throw of the dice in terms of winning a world championship.

What is not in doubt is the fact that financially Dave's boxing career was an outstanding success, and although Arthur Boggis has come in for criticism throughout, he contributed in no small measure to this conclusion. It was Boggis who arranged the fights and the purses right until the end, and they both thrived. From press reports at the time it can be estimated that from Dave's first seventeen fights he would have earned in the region of £1,500. Using the retail price index this would equate to about £25,000 at today's value. He probably earned the same in 1956, but then his earning shot upwards. Between 1957 and 1960 Dave grossed around £32,000, or over £600,000 today. Between 1960 and his final fight with Griffith it can be estimated Dave earned around £1 million using the same multiplier. He did have outlays of course, the managers cut was always 25% and training fees were usually around a further 10%. As we've seen with his new home and hairdressing business, he did not waste his hard earned cash, and this was used to fund future successes beyond his boxing career.

Historical Note – 1964
Top of the Pops broadcast for the first time
Great Train Robbers are sentenced to 307 years
Announcement of plans to build the World Trade Centre in New York
BBC 2 launched
Olympic Games held in Tokyo
Forth Road bridge opens and Post Office tower reaches its maximum height

CHAPTER 15

Life After Boxing

The vast majority of professional boxers cannot rely solely on their income from fighting to sustain their daily lives. When their career ends life carries on relatively undisturbed. For others, who are more successful, they still don't earn enough during the short lifespan their career lasts, to ensure that they never need to take another job. The exceptions are the *superstars* of the sport who become very wealthy indeed and never need to worry about where their next penny is coming from. In 1965, Dave Charnley fell into this latter category.

Some ex-boxers do manage to forge out new and lucrative careers for themselves. Mickey Duff, for example, moved from being a boxer into matchmaking and then became a boxing promoter. Sir Henry Cooper became a media celebrity while maintaining a shop he bought while still fighting. Jim Watt has become a well known and respected boxing commentator, as has Barry McGuigan. The Fen Tiger, Dave 'Boy' Green became a successful businessman, so too did Tony Sibson. Dave Charnley is one of the fortunate few who went on to be as successful away from the ring as he was in it.

Of course Dave, like his contemporary Henry Cooper, had made plans for life after boxing when he opened up his hairdressers shop. This business proved to be very lucrative and turned out to have been a shrewd investment. In fact, if he had done nothing else but maintain this interest, it is likely that a comfortable lifestyle would have been assured. But Dave, with a similar drive to that which made his boxing career so successful, branched out in a completely different direction.

While still boxing he had met and made friends with many people locally who would subsequently provide significant help and guidance at just the right time. This fact alone justifies the assertion that Dave didn't let the fame effect his basic quiet and modest character. Why else would people willingly assist him?

The mid 1960s were proving to be a boom time for house building and home ownership. The austerity of the war years was starting to fade into the distant past. Industry were expanding and a new middle class had been created which valued wealth, and the outward signs of that wealth. New cars and new houses had become the ultimate status symbols. Dave is fortunate that some of his friends were involved in the building trade and it is also fortunate that Dave recognised an opportunity when he saw it.

A local builder Ben Williams sold him land at Horton Kirby and employing other friends, Jimmy Fishenden, another builder, and Joe Storey who looked after financial matters, Dave built in the region of a dozen homes. Dave had no previous experience of this trade but he made sure he learned quickly, and soon realised that he wanted an emphasis placed on quality. He was determined that his houses would be worth the money people were paying for them. Even today he emphasises that he wanted buyers to be completely satisfied with their purchases, and he had a desire to establish a reputation based on value for money.

Dave was careful not to over extend himself and wouldn't move onto a new site until the houses were all sold on an existing project. Very quickly other estates emerged including those at Joydens Wood, Albert Road in Bexley, Baldwyn's Park and the largest at Newbarn in Dartford, this latter site containing over thirty five houses. Dave Charnley Estates Limited was incorporated in February 1965 and the business went from success to success. However, Dave's efforts during his boxing career and his enthusiasm for this new venture were beginning to take their toll on his marriage to Ruth.

Dave had met Ruth when she was fourteen years old and he was only two years her senior. Five years later they were married and during his boxing career they were virtually inseparable. The couple lived at Thanet Road in Bexley until they moved to *Greenwood* a designer home in Darenth Road in Dartford some seven years later. It seems that within a couple of years of his building business taking off the couple were starting to drift apart. Life must have been so different then from the days when the young local girl and the apprentice boilermaker set up home.

When they eventually separated and went their own ways their new luxury bungalow, *Brooklands Park*, was put up for sale and Dave moved into a flat above his hairdressers shop in Spital Street, Dartford, accommodation which also included a small office. It was during this period that Dave struck up a firm friendship with former sparring partner George Cottle and his wife Maureen, who were the proprietors of the Red Cow pub in Bermondsey. They became the greatest of companions even going on holiday every summer to Cannes. Not many women would have accepted their husband's pal coming with them on their annual holidays, but Maureen wouldn't have had it any other way. George and Maureen remained Dave's closest friends until George's sad passing a few years ago.

After a couple of years in his bachelor pad, Dave moved out briefly to Ash Road in nearby Hartley, but his heart was set on building another *dream* house, this time for himself. That house was built on Kingsingfield Road, West Kingsdown near Sevenoaks, and in deference to his family's heritage he called it *Craigneuk*. This property today, which according to internet sites is valued in the region of £ 1.2 million, must have been a symbol to Dave of how far the Charnley and Fraser family had come since that daring move in the mid 1930s which brought his mother and father from Scotland to Dartford. Dave went a stage further in his efforts to formally record his respect for his family by naming two streets at Coldblow on Dartford Road, Bexley, Helen Close and Fraser Close, after his beloved mother.

Also towards the end of the 1960s, with so much of Dave's attention being devoted to house building, his involvement in the hairdressing business began to diminish. There was a trend emerging on High Streets which saw the acquisition of family run shops by national conglomerates. Dave took the opportunity, with a touch of regret, to sell his hairdressers shop to one such enterprise. He'd had the shop for around eight years and it had earned him some *tongue in cheek* wisecracks from the press who enjoyed the fact that Britain's favourite boxer had taken this unusual step. Dave certainly had a laugh –all the way to the bank!

Another aspect of Dave's life, which was slightly out of the norm for retired sportsmen, was his ability to remain fit looking and around his *fighting weight.* Photographs from that era show him in a good light and although he still occasionally had time for an early morning run his weight was kept in check by his eating habits and his new pastime of playing squash. He used to eat small amounts often, long before it became an apparently healthy eating habit favoured by high profile dieticians. Maureen Cottle remarks that she has seldom seen Dave ever finish a meal. Whether this healthy eating habit was something that came natural to him is open to debate but it must surely have found its roots in the strict diets he undertook during his boxing career. In addition to his eating habits older brother William remembers another possible reason for his good shape. William once met an Egyptian who played top level squash. He told William that although Dave didn't have great technique he could keep pace with him longer than most of those he competed against. It is likely that there was a third reason why Dave stayed in trim and unfortunately it was one he was not proud of – he started smoking! William, among others, couldn't understand it, and when he challenged Dave to explain how someone who had been so dedicated to his fitness could go down that particular route, Dave could only say that he needed to keep himself occupied by doing something with his hands.

For a few years after he retired Dave would still be invited to the big boxing shows in London usually involving the fights of Henry Cooper and later on, Joe Bugner. Very often he would travel up to London with brother Joe just like they used to do when Dave first started out. Joe remembers that it became a habit on those occasions to stop off at the Beaverwood Club in Sidcup where they would round off the night. Dave always made himself available to attend award ceremonies, and opening functions, for a wide range of organisations usually related in some way to boxing. Although still shy and reluctant to make speeches he nevertheless was well received and his personal attendances were universally appreciated.

In the early 1970s Dave met Bernie Green a man who became a close personal friend and who would provide Dave with new business opportunities in London. Dave met Bernie one night when they were socialising at a restaurant in St Martin's Lane. Bernie recognised Dave from his days as a boxer and introduced himself. They kept bumping into each other and eventually became firm friends. They ended up buying property next to each other in Devonshire Place Mews adjacent to Harley Street. They re-designed this property into enviable accommodation and when Dave sold *Craigneuk* he moved into this house for a spell.

In 1974 the BBC contacted Dave with a view to filming a programme on boxing. Feeling he needed a bit of advice on his presentation, he turned to a friend David Hill, an Editor with the Weekend Mail magazine. Dave went to a meeting with his advisor accompanied by ever reliable friend, George Cottle. Dave eventually decided against going ahead with the programme as he wasn't happy with the type of questions he was going to be asked. However the meeting was a bit of a *set-up*, because his friends had arranged for a young lady to join them in the hope that Dave and her would hit it off. Well the mutual attraction was instant and the group moved on to Annabel's where George's wife Maureen joined them. The young lady was Maureen Workman. Maureen was a fashion model who'd had small parts in the first version of the film Casino Royale and several television programmes including Dr Who. This chance meeting led to a romance which is still strong some 37 years, and two daughters later.

Soon after they met, Maureen remembers a strange encounter. While enjoying a meal with Dave at the Tiberio restaurant in Queen Street an older man approached Dave and said, 'I know you wouldn't come to me, so I'm coming to speak to you'. He then asked if he could sit down for a few minutes. It was clear to Maureen that they both knew each other well, but unusually, Dave wouldn't look at him and the conversation was very frosty. After the man left their company and returned to his own table, Maureen asked who he was. Dave simply replied, 'It was Arthur Boggis, he was my manager when I was boxing'.

Maureen and David were married in the registry office at Caxton Hall, Victoria in 1976 with Bernie Green performing duties as the best man. They then moved on to the 21 Club to join family and friends for lunch before ending the night at a club in the West End. By this time Dave had made the leap from Dartford to London and had taken up an office in North Audley Street near Grosvenor Square. To allow Dave to be near his workplace the couple started out married life together at his Mews in Devonshire Place. It was there that daughter Lisa was born but much as they both loved this accommodation they both concluded that it was not ideal for a family, and with this in mind they moved back out of London briefly to Swanley Village in Kent where second daughter Joanna was welcomed into the world. They soon after settled at Manor Drive in Hartley which was to be the family home for the next 24 years.

Dave Charnley Estates was going from strength to strength, so much so that Dave had to move to larger office space in Regent Street. By this time Dave was indulging his weakness for cars and could now be seen driving into work from Hartley in his shining new Rolls Royce, leaving behind his E-type Jaguar for weekend work!

Through Bernie Green, Dave made important contacts and expanded Dave Charnley Estates into the refurbishment sector of the market, working with among others Taylor Woodrow and Regional Properties. Dave by now had a lucrative contract with the latter company who owned several office blocks in and around central London. As a floor of offices in these buildings came up for modernisation Dave would move in using his own full time staff and sub-contracted workmen. It was usually the case that as one group of offices were completed another would be ready for similar treatment, and this rolling programme of work made it a profitable enterprise.

Dave's successful boxing career, and his continued progress in the world of commerce, allowed him to provide their daughters with the best possible start in life. Both Lisa and Joanna attended a private preparatory school in Hartley before moving on to St Hilary's (later Walthamstowe Hall) in Sevenoaks. The girls remember their dad as a stickler for effort, and accuracy, in their homework. His attention to detail even went to the extent of him having to ensure that their pencils were always sharpened!

Dave was a regular visitor to the most popular establishments in the West End. The *21 Club*, *Langans* and *Les Ambassadeurs* enjoyed his patronage and he was on speaking terms with many of the celebrities of the day including Terry Venables, George Best, Malcolm Allison and Jimmy Tarbuck. On one occasion in Langans, while sitting waiting for friends to arrive, Dave was asked by the manager if he would mind if a visitor sat with him until a table became free. Dave was stunned when Al Pacino walked over. He was even more surprised when the American film star began discussing Dave's boxing career and afterwards when recounting the tale to his family he told them he felt as if he had been on a film set.

By the late 80s the house building business around Dartford was starting to fade. Most of the available plots of land had been snapped up and any which did emerge were usually bought by the national building companies. At the same time, Dave's major client, Regional Properties, changed hands and Dave lost his major re-furbishing contract. Nevertheless, it was around this period that Dave was introduced to Alan Parnell who would become a lifelong friend. Alan was soon to become the Chief Engineer at one of Hilton International's hotels in London. Mutual friend, Mike Dillon, who owned Gerry's Club in Dean Street, brought them together because he knew Alan was looking for a reputable company to carry out building and refurbishment work. Alan remembers that Dave had two companies by then, Dave Charnley Estates and Dave Charnley Modernisation. They immediately took to one another, and Dave carried out work for Alan on a regular basis throughout the next 10 years. Although Dave's companies did all types of work, he had gained an enviable reputation in the trade for the quality of his decorating work. Dave's firm were always in demand and he had contracts at several prestigious properties in Knightsbridge and Mayfair. Alan remembers Dave regularly visiting his sites to ensure that work was progressing satisfactorily and to the expected standard. No matter how busy Alan and Dave were however, they always found time on Fridays to get away from work, to socialise, usually in the Fox House and then Fino's before finally settling down in Langans.

As Dave was approaching another milestone, his 60th birthday in 1995, wife Maureen suggested a party, but typically for Dave, he rejected the idea out of hand. Nevertheless, outwith Dave's knowledge, William's wife Eileen took responsibility for the arrangements and decided that her own house in Wilmington would be the venue. Maureen started making contact with family and friends from near and far. Sister Isabella, a long term resident in Florida, indicated that she would not be able to attend, creating a cloud over festivities. But, unknown to everyone except George and Maureen Cottle, she had indeed arrived in the UK during the week leading up to the party and had based herself in their hotel. The guests all arrived in Wilmington early and parked their cars at a neighbour's house. Maureen had persuaded Dave to agree to a small family meal at his brother and sister in law's house, and was totally lost for words when he saw all the old friends who had gathered there. A bigger surprise was to follow for everyone. Isabel phoned the house and spoke to Dave, apologising for not making it over. At the same time, she walked into the lounge and while Dave took some very hard punches during his career, he could have been knocked over with a feather on this occasion! Ex-sparring partner, and former Star referee Larry O'Connell, made a very personal speech in which he recounted quotes from many writers during Dave's boxing career, most notably Reg Gutteridge. Another highlight for Dave was the opportunity, for the first time, to see some of his fights on video. Brother William had engaged his friend, and former promoter, Mickey Duff, to track down old fight films through his contacts in the media. Mickey was also a welcome guest at the celebrations and he was on hand to answer queries about Dave's career from those too young to remember.

At the turn of the new century, with Dave having reached retirement age, he decided the time had come to wind down his business interests. With daughters, Lisa and Joanna, now working in the media, and living away from home, Dave and Maureen left their house in Hartley and moved to West Malling. They still enjoy a social evening with friends in the city as well as visiting the girls in South London and Manchester. Maureen Cottle remains a very close friend.

It is doubtful that Dave's neighbours today would have any idea that he was such a major sports star all those years ago. His daughters have rarely heard their father talk of his boxing career. They used to feel very proud, when the family, while out socially, would be approached by perfect strangers intent on speaking to their father. Both the girls and their mother used to wonder why someone, who had been so successful, would want to shut this part of their life out almost completely. But in later years they feel they have found the answer.

Dave, according to his family, is such a perfectionist. Everything has to be done with maximum effort, and he gets frustrated when people don't try their hardest. In many ways *second best* is simply not good enough. The consensus view of the family is that because Dave didn't win the world title, he feels that he was in some way a failure. That everything else he achieved in boxing is worthless, and therefore not worth discussing. This view is supported in some way by Dave surprisingly putting up his coveted Lonsdale Belt and Empire title trophy for auction in 2006. Although those closest to him were deeply saddened by this unexpected turn of events, Dave himself seemed to be totally unaffected. For the vast majority of us who lead a fairly bland, routine sort of existence, we may find this mindset difficult to understand.

Dave Charnley, the Dartford Destroyer, was not a failure. He retired as undefeated British lightweight champion having held the title for over seven years. He was undefeated European champion a title he did not lose in the ring. He won the ABA title by knocking out the best amateur boxer Britain has ever produced. From 1957 until 1962 he was the biggest star in British boxing. Hold your head up Dave, for those who saw you fight at your peak, you were, in their eyes, a real world champion!

An Opponent's View

Brian Curvis

I was so proud when I knew I would be fighting Dave Charnley. In my opinion he was the best lightweight this country has ever produced. When I fought Dave he was the most famous boxer in Britain, even more famous than Henry Cooper.

I knew beforehand that the promoter Jack Solomons was lining up a fight between Dave and Emile Griffith for the world welterweight title. I also knew that Jack would not get permission for Dave to fight Griffith from the British Boxing Board, so he thought that if Dave beat me, seeing I was the British welterweight champion, they couldn't refuse.

During the fight I kept moving to my left to get away from Dave's left hooks, and I always tried to stay close to him so he couldn't get the full power into his punches. He only caught me once, and when he did I was knocked down, and I was lucky to get to my feet. Everybody knew he was a terrific puncher coming forward, but he was not so good on his back foot.

I was always sorry I didn't get to know Dave better, but he was so quiet, he didn't talk much. I knew that his manager Arthur Boggis sorted out good paydays for him, because he didn't commit him to fighting for any single promoter.

I went on to fight Griffith for the world title, and this fight shouldn't have went ahead as I was suffering from internal stomach bleeding a few days before. I know Dave lost badly to Griffith a few months later but that was not the real Dave

Charnley who fought that night. I don't know what was wrong with him, but Griffith should not have been able to beat the Dave Charnley I knew like that.

Dave Charnley was great fighter, a very big puncher for his weight, and it was an honour to fight him.

The Family View

Joe Charnley, Dave's Brother

When our much loved mother died age 38 in February 1950 our family of three brothers and a young sister became very close and protective of each other. So it was not easy to watch one of us being hit by somebody else which is obviously what happens on a regular basis if you practice what is known as the noble art. We do not personally get hurt but we felt every blow. Also the nerves took over and I at least had to ensure I knew the quickest way to the toilet when the contest started. This torture began in the late forties and early fifties when Dave and myself were members of the Dartford Boxing Club. I soon discovered that I was better at fighting shadows than real people so I dropped out and left it to the real boxer. My brother Dave, myself and my brother William, and my late father spent the next fifteen years supporting him everywhere he fought. The early years as a schoolboy champion at arenas all over London and the Home Counties. To the South East divisional to London championships at the Albert Hall. He of course won all these and qualified for the amateur boxing finals at Wembley in April 1954. He reached the final where he destroyed Dick McTaggart inside 70 seconds. McTaggart as we know went on to win an Olympic gold medal. We did not have long to celebrate as he announced he would be turning professional. It was no surprise to me as I knew his intentions. The amateur authorities wanted him to compete at the next Olympics where they thought him an obvious gold medal winner but he had made up his mind and had his first professional bout in October 1954 which he won easily. He then fought on a regular basis all over the country getting more experience with every fight until he qualified to fight for the British lightweight title held at the time by a very good fighter called Joe Lucy. David won the fight and the British title. He went on to win the European and commonwealth championships as well.

During this period he had also been fighting and beating many of the leading contenders for the world title and in 1961 the match was made for Dave to fight for the world title against one of the great champions American Joe Brown. The bout at Earls Court was attended by almost 20,000 people, the most to have attended an indoor event at this time. The fight over fifteen rounds went as I had imagined with Dave doing most of the work and Brown being wiley and experience keeping him out of harms way. At the end myself and almost the entire crowd thought Dave had won it but a misguided and myopic referee, to the astonishment of everyone including Brown held up the champions hand. The booing and demonstrations were long and loud but no matter, the damage was done. Dave in the next few years fought and beat all the leading contenders for the title and was in line for another title fight. It is my opinion and mine only, that the spark and ambition had diminished and he retired in 1964. He then had several business interests outside of boxing and other fish to fry. When reading this book you will get more information regarding his career and his efforts and determination during this time but I hope you will also come to see the quiet and unassuming man that he is, without a trace of ego despite his obvious achievements.

I am extremely proud of him.

Isabella Charnley, Dave's Sister

My first memories of David being a fighter were that he was always training and I remember very well that his training clothes were always in front of the coal fire in the living room to make sure that they were dry for the next day – no such luxury as clothes dryers in those days.

I can remember all his trips abroad when he represented England as an amateur – I could never wait for him to get home because he always brought me back a present – I remember one of my favorites was a doll in Dutch National Dress – boy were the girls at school jealous of that.

I remember my dad and stepmother organising buses to go to the fights – it was so exciting and I don't believe anybody had seen anything like it before – I can remember people walking in the street waving to us and cars honking their horns. I remember going up the Old Kent Road and past the Thomas A Beckett, the pub where some of the greatest fighters from all over the world came to train.

As a youngster I could never appreciate just how good our David was – but of course as I got older it became clear that he was very special and was in fact a very talented and dedicated athlete.

The greatest disappointment was that David was robed of the world title against Joe Brown – that's not just me saying that, that was the opinion of most of the most famous sports writers and boxing experts of the day.

I remember coming home on the bus that night and his fans were devastated – I even saw grown men cry because he had lost. But to this day I have never heard David complain about that decision. He took it like a man and the great sportsman that he was.

Even to this day I can get goose pimples when I remember the overwhelming pride I would feel when the fanfare would start and the two fighters would enter the ring – when it was David's turn the crowds would go mad and raise the roof with cheers. Great memories!

David should be remembered as a dedicated disciplined fighter who gave his all in every fight that he had – when they saw a Dave Charnley fight – fans always got the best he could give.

William Charnley, Dave's Brother

I would like to thank the author of my brother David's biography for giving me the opportunity to say something about him.

I was with him the day we discovered the Scouts Hall in Little Queen Street, Dartford, run by an old time fighter Bob Lloyd. We had arrived from our home in Craigneuk, Scotland, two naïve kids wide-eyed with enthusiasm. Bob asked us in and with the sixpence that our grandmother had given us, we joined the club.

There has always been confusion about David's nationality. So let me clear it up. I was born in Scotland in 1932 and in 1935 our parents went to Dartford to seek work. My mother was pregnant and gave birth to David shortly afterwards, but we always considered ourselves Scottish. The whole Charnley family from Craigneuk came too. It was at the behest of our Uncle Sam, a professional footballer that had captained Wolverhampton Wanderers in the English League who at the end of his career had moved to Dartford to play further in the Southern League and was a well-liked man. Some of the directors of Dartford Football Club were local businessmen and gave my father and uncle jobs in their factories. They couldn't believe their luck as they had been out of work for years. The war came and we were bombed out of our house on the Brent, which had been badly damaged with every door and window blasted out. So we returned to Scotland to live in our home village of Craigneuk – an amazing place for mainly boxers and footballers. I could name 35 professional footballers and numerous boxers, three of whom fought for the Championship of the World and retired Undefeated Champions of Great Britain, Europe and the British Empire - a remarkable record for a small area. We returned to England after the war and David walked into the Scouts Hall and was an immediate success. He was a kid with extraordinary talent. I am sure that Jim Kirkwood has fully dealt with his career and I will not go into that. But, I have to say that David was the most modest fighter; he never boasted in his life about what he did or what he could do. He never complained about the bad decisions given against him and always praised his opponent. I am extremely proud of him for that, because I know I couldn't have.

I will give you one incident of David's dry sense of humour. He had fought Joe Brown for the Lightweight Championship of the World at Earls Court in front of 18,000 people and the vast majority thought that David had won, including the sports writers. In the dressing room, David sat on a chair with his hands in a bucket of water and a towel over his head; the whole room was silent and nobody knew what to say. In walked an Irish promoter who put his arm around David's shoulders and said "It's a disgrace David; he hardly touched you through the whole fight". David took the towel off his head to show a very bruised face and a cut the whole length of his nose and said, "Who the hell did this?!" The whole room burst into laughter. This is the man I remember, and was extremely proud of him and honoured to be his brother and still am.

Dave Charnley Amateur Record from October 1952 until September 1954

Date	Venue	Opponent	Result
11 November	Mile End	H Farquar	W pts
11 December	Mile End	J Culwick	W KO 3
12 December	Chiswick	A Drew	L pts
14 December	Eltham	W Norman	W pts
1953			
7 January	Hackney	A Drew	W pts
22 January	Walworth	M O'Connor	W KO 3
22 January	Walworth	L Mills	W pts
22 January	Walworth	T Haddon	W pts
(Winner of 9th Novices Competition)			
2 February	Dartford	R Hope	W KO 2
19 February	Woolwich	W Hurley	W pts
26 February	Walworth	A Stephens	W pts
9 March	Eltham	C Chatham	W KO 1
9 March	Eltham	W Norman	W KO 2
10 March	Eltham	P Dempster	W Disq 3
(South East London Division Featherweight Champion)			
25 March	Empress Hall	A Drew	W pts
25 March	Empress Hall	P Lewis	L pts
(London Division Featherweight Runner-up)			
1 April	Walworth	A Stephens	W pts
20 April	Mile End	D Steff	W pts

23 May	Shepherds Bush	B Roger (Belgian champion)	W pts
	(Hammersmith Select v Belgium)		
4 June	Clapham	P Duffell	W pts
(London ABA v RAF)			
12 June	Amsterdam	J Van d. Zee (Dutch champion)	W pts
(London ABA v Amsterdam)			
26 September	Frankfurt	H P Mehling	W pts
	(Great Britain v West Germany)		
29 September	Fulda	E Schnaber (West German champion)	W pts
10 October	Royal Albert Hall	T Butler	W disq. 2
	(London ABA v Dublin and Leinster)		
28 October	Wembley	C Hamia	L pts
	(Great Britain v France)		
3 November	Mile End	R Baldwin	W KO 2
11 November	Walworth	T Nicholls	L pts
12 December	Bethnal Green	B Neill	W pts
16 December	Bermondsey	J Leach	W KO 2

1954

1 January	Dartford	R Jones	W KO 3
26 January	Glasgow	T Ball	W pts
5 February	Berlin	H Stutz	W KO 3
	(London ABA v Berlin)		
22 February	Walworth	F Woodman	W pts
6 March	Eltham	R Warnes	W KO 2

(South East London Division qualifier)

8 March	Eltham	L Mills	W KO 3
(South East London Division Featherweight Champion)			
15 April	Royal Albert Hall	F Woodman	W disq. 2
(London Divisional Finals)			
15 April	Royal Albert Hall	A Drew	W disq. 1
(London Division Featherweight Champion)			
23 April	Wembley	M Collins	W pts
(ABA semi-final)			
23 April	Wembley	D McTaggart	W KO 1
(ABA champion)			
29 April	Mile End	J Culwick	W KO 1
28 May	Royal Albert Hall	K Thomas	W KO 1
(Great Britain v Imperial Services)			
1 August	Vancouver	G Durey (Australia)	W rsf 2
(Empire Games)			
5 August	Vancouver	L Leisching	L pts
(Bronze Medal Winner)			

Dave Charnley Professional Record

Date	Venue	Opponent	Result
1954			
19 October	London	Malcolm Ames	W rsf 3
12 November	Blackpool	Percy James	W Ko 2
23 November	London	Roy Paine	W pts 6
7 December	London	Pat McCoy	W rsf 6
1955			
7 January	Blackpool	Andy Monahan	W Ko 1
27 January	London	Nye Ankrah	W Ko 1
8 February	London	Neville Tetlow	W Ko 2
17 February	Liverpool	Willie Lloyd	D 8
22 March	London	Denny Dawson	W disq 7
24 May	London	Jeff Walters	W disq 6
9 June	Birmingham	Johnny Mann	W pts 8
26 July	Birmingham	Teddy Best	W pts 8
3 October	Nottingham	Stan Skinkiss	W rsf 4
13 October	London	Jackie Butler	W rsf 4
1 November	London	Leo Molloy	W pts 8
15 November	London	Guy Gracia	L pts 10
28 November	Nottingham	Kurt Ernest	W rsf 6
1956			
6 March	London	Johnny Butterworth	W rsf 5
3 April	London	Sammy McCarthy	W pts 10

19 June	London	Fernand Coppens	W rsf 2
24 July	Dartford	Johnny Miller	W rtd 6
27 August	Cardiff	Willie Lloyd	L pts 10
16 November	Manchester	Alby Tissong	W pts 8

1957

22 January	London	Willie Lloyd	W rsf 12
(Eliminator for British Lightweight Title)			
9 April	London	Joe Lucy	W pts 15
(British Lightweight Title)			
4 June	London	Johnny Gonsalves	W rsf 8
9 July	London	Willie Toweel	L pts 15
(British Empire Lightweight Title)			
30 September	Southampton	Joe Woussem	W rsf 10
19 November	London	Ron Hinson	W pts 10

1958

28 January	London	Don Jordan	W pts 10
11 March	London	Tony Garcia	W rsf 5
15 April	London	Peter Waterman	W rsf 5
3 June	London	Joe Lopes	W pts 10
18 September	Liverpool	Jimmy Croll	W ret 4
28 October	London	Carlos Ortiz	L pts 10

1959

10 March	London	Guy Gracia	L pts 10
12 May	London	Willie Toweel	W Ko 10
(British Empire Lightweight Title)			
17 June	Glasgow	Billy Kelly	W disq 6

4 September	London	Jimmy Brown	W rsf 8
2 December	Houston, Texas	Joe Brown	L ret 5
	(World Lightweight Title)		
1960			
23 February	London	Saveur Benamou	W pts 10
29 March	London	Mario Vecchiatto	W ret 10
	(European Lightweight Title)		
31 May	London	Paul Armstead	W Ko 9
1961			
17 January	London	Gene Gresham	W pts 10
21 February	London	Fernand Nollett	W pts 15
	(European lightweight title)		
18 April	London	Joe Brown	L pts 15
	(World Lightweight Title)		
5 July	Rome	Raymondo Nobile	W ret 4
	(European lightweight title)		
5 September	London	Lenny Matthews	W pts 10
20 November	Nottingham	David Hughes	W Ko 1
	(British Lightweight Title)		
27 November	Manchester	L C Morgan	W Ko 3
1962			
30 January	Liverpool	Jose Stable	W pts 10
5 June	London	Doug Vaillant	L pts 10
4 August	Kingston, Jamaica	Bunny Grant	L pts 15
	(British Empire Lightweight Title)		

11 December	London	J D Ellis	W rsf 6
1963			
15 January	London	Jethro Cason	W pts 10
25 February	Manchester	Joe Brown	W Ko 6
20 May	Manchester	Maurice Cullen	W pts 15
	(British Lightweight Title)		
25 November	Manchester	Tito Marshall	L pts 10
1964			
24 March	London	Brian Curvis	L pts 10
2 June	London	Kenny Lane	W pts 10
1 December	London	Emile Griffith	L rsf 9